CHRIST AS CONQUEROR AND RECONCILER

CHRIST AS CONQUEROR AND RECONCILER

THEOLOGICAL IMPLICATIONS *for the* CHURCH'S ROLE *in* DELIVERANCE

A Study of Colossians
1:19-20 and 2:13-15

JAMES E. NORWOOD, Sr.

Word & Spirit Press
Tulsa, Oklahoma

Christ as Conqueror and Reconciler: Theological Implications for the Church's Role in Deliverance: A Study of Colossians 1:19–20 and 2:13–15

Copyright © 2008 by James Edward Norwood, Sr.

All rights reserved. Written permission must be secured from the publisher to use or reproduce any part of this book except for brief quotations in critical reviews or articles. Printed in the United States of America

Published in Tulsa, Oklahoma, by Word & Spirit Press

WordSP@gmail.com
http://WandSP.com

Book design and composition by Bob Bubnis / Booksetters, Bowling Green, Kentucky

ISBN 10: 0-9785352-4-3 [case laminate]
ISBN 13: 978-0-9785352-4-7

∞ The paper used in this publication meets the minimum requirements of the American National Standard for Information Sciences—Permanence of Paper for Printed Library Materials, ANSI Z39.48-1992.

Cover illustration: Eugène Delacroix, Christ on the Cross (sketch), 1845; Oil on wood, 37 x 25 cm, Museum Boijmans Van Beuningen, Rotterdam

DEDICATION

To the memory of my beloved, late parents,
Foster M. Norwood, Sr., and *Annie V. Norwood*,
for instilling in me the importance of enduring
and sacrificing until tasks are completed

To my loving and supportive wife, *Laura Ruth*

and to
our children

James E. Jr.
Jarrinetta
Donn Nathan
Michael Andrew
Diana Ruth

ACKNOWLEDGMENTS

I am convinced that books are not written in isolation, but in community. That is certainly no less true of this book. I could not have completed it without the assistance of many others along the way—family, teachers, supervisors, consultants, colleagues, and friends. Dr. M. Robert Mansfield, Dr. Cheryl Iverson, and Dr. Mark Hall gently shepherded this project from its inception to its completion as a master's thesis at Oral Roberts University. The process of transforming it into a book helps me to realize and appreciate more fully their influence on this work; their guidance will long be remembered.

Special gratitude goes to Dr. Thomson Mathew, Dean of the ORU School of Theology and Missions, for allowing me as much time as possible to get the project completed. I also appreciate my friends and colleagues deeply, especially Dr. Trevor Grizzle and Dr. James Tollett, for their prayers and support.

ORU Librarians Ms. Myra Bloom and Ms. Peggy Pixley receive my gratitude for their expert library assistance. I further express appreciation to Ms. Evelyn Turner, my former Administrative Secretary, and to Ms. Marlene Mankins, my current Administrative Secretary, for their invaluable assistance.

Finally, I sincerely thank Dr. Mark E. Roberts, who is an expert literary agent and colleague, and his design partner, Mr. Bob Bubnis of BookSetters, for their willingness to take on this project and enhance its quality and style as a book.

SUMMARY

This study shows the close relationship between the portrayal of Christ as Reconciler of hostile beings, or powers, in Colossians 1:19-20 and His depiction as Conqueror over them in Colossians 2:13-15. It examines each portrayal exegetically—separately and then jointly. Next, it draws out theological implications for the Church's role in deliverance—cosmically and individually.

The study affirms that Christ fulfilled both of these roles because the fullness of God abides in Him and because God works through Christ's death on the cross. Both of these criteria make it possible for Christ to reconcile all things—cosmically and individually—to Himself and be victorious—cosmically and individually—over all His enemies.

Because of His reconciling and victorious work—cosmically and individually, one can individually experience deliverance from evil beings, powers, or forces now. He or she is encouraged through the Church to continue this ministry, waiting for the fuller manifestation of it at the consummation of the ages.

CONTENTS

Acknowledgments vii
Summary ix
Preface xiii

Part I

Chapter 1. Introduction 1
    The Colossian Church and Heresy 2
    Christ as Conqueror 7
    Christ as Reconciler 10
    Rationale for the Research 14
    Definition of Terms 15
    Summary 17

Part II

Chapter 2. The Fullness of God in Christ: The Reconciler (Colossians 1:19-20) 21
    The Fullness of Christ: Colossians 1:19 23
    Christ as Reconciler: Colossians 1:20 27

Chapter 3. The Fullness of God in Christ: The Forgiver and Conqueror (Colossians 2:13-15) 35
    Christ as Forgiver: Colossians 2:13 37
    Christ as Conqueror: Colossians 2:14 39
    Christ as Conqueror: Colossians 2:15 46

Part III

Chapter 4. Theological Implications for Deliverance 59
Chapter 5. The Church's Role in Deliverance 69

Summary and Conclusion of the Study..................................77
Bibliography..79
Greek Index 85
Scripture Index...87
Author Index..91
Subject Index..93
About the Author 105

PREFACE

The impetus for this study was kindled by several areas of concern. First, since I have taught a class titled "Abnormal Human Behavior" for several years and am aware that various addictions, which are forms of bondage, are growing problems in society today, I am personally interested in addressing these problems. Some psychologists tend to view these addictions only from a naturalistic perspective and as something that happens to persons from within and for which they have lost the ability to reason with themselves,[1] or they are due to "elevated levels of a common substance in the brain called dopamine."[2] The success rate for recovery from addictions is generally very low and recidivism is very high.[3] This suggests that there are possibly other factors from without[4] that may be influencing addictions. Such forces may not be accounted for by a naturalistic view, which is a product of the "enlightened" worldview that has pervaded Western culture for the last several hundred years.[5]

Second, it is known that some addictions are influenced or caused by spiritual beings or forces that may oppress and perhaps even possess a person, for which deliverance would be more appropriate than naturalistic therapy in addressing

---

1 Abraham J. Twerski, *Addictive Thinking: Understanding Self-Deception*, 2d ed. (Center City, MN: Hazelden Foundation, 1997), 38.
2 J. Madeleine Nash, "The Chemistry of Addiction," *Time*, 5 May 1997, 69.
3 Nash, 76.
4 Frank Stagg, *New Testament Theology* (Nashville, TN: Broadman Press, 1962), 23.
5 Gregory Boyd, *God at War: The Bible & Spiritual Conflict* (Downers Grove, IL: InterVarsity Press, 1997), 238.

the problems.⁶ The churches, especially some mainline Protestant churches, have, since the Enlightenment, tended to shun this way of perceiving problems of bondage and have relegated them to the secular realm. This way of viewing the problems was not the worldview of almost all other cultures throughout history, and neither is it the worldview of more of the West as well, as it enters postmodernity more fully.⁷ In fact, Jesus and his earliest disciples believed that the universe was filled with "spiritual beings, some good and some evil, which were at war with one another."⁸

Finally, while taking a class titled "The Cross/Resurrection in the New Testament," a course in my biblical literature M.A. program, I discovered that some scholars are addressing the problems to some extent, identifying the cross as the locus of God's power that makes deliverance from bondage possible. But biblical literature still lacks sufficient study of the concepts of Christ as conqueror and reconciler from exegetical and theological perspectives, with emphasis on the theological implications for deliverance and the Church's role in it as a viable form of ministry of the Church today. This study aims to help fill this void in scholarship for the purpose of Gospel ministry.

---

6 Frederick F. Bruce, "Colossian Problems, Part 4: Christ as Conqueror and Reconciler," *Bibliotheca Sacra* 141 (1984): 299. *ATLA Religious Database*, EBSCOhost (13 October 2005).
7 Boyd, 238.
8 Boyd, 238.

Part I

Chapter One

Introduction

There is a growing problem with various addictions in society today. The churches, especially some mainline Protestant denominations, tend to avoid or relegate the causes of these addictions to the secular realm only, rather than perceiving that some of them may be caused by personal spiritual beings or impersonal spiritual forces for which deliverance may be more appropriate as a form of treatment. Some biblical scholars are addressing, to various degrees, the problem of "addiction or bondage" to spiritual beings or forces. No study, however, was found that dealt, separately and jointly, with the similarities and differences between the concepts of Christ as Reconciler (Col 1:19-20)[1] and as Conqueror (Col 2:13-15) from both exegetical and theological perspectives, with emphasis on the theological implications for the Church's role in deliverance. Hence, the primary purpose of this study is to show the similarities and differences between Christ's function in these two roles. A secondary purpose is to assess these two concepts in light of their theological implications for the Church's role in deliverance—cosmically and individually.

---

[1] Unless otherwise indicated all Bible references in this paper are to the *Updated New American Standard Bible* (UNASB) (La Habra, CA: The Lockman Foundation, 1995).

Christ as Conqueror and Reconciler

THE COLOSSIAN CHURCH AND HERESY

There is no documentation on the establishment of the church at Colossae. In fact, all the information about the church is derived from what is written in the letter. Three things may possibly be said, based upon what is written. First, the preaching of the gospel and planting of churches in the Lycus Valley were, from all indications, the work of Epaphras, who was called by Paul a "fellow bond-servant" (Col 1:7) and "fellow prisoner" (Phlm 23;[2] also cf. 1:8; 2:1; 4:12, 13). Epaphras was probably a convert of Paul's and, in the evangelization of Colossae, was acting as representative of him (cf. Col 1:7, 8). The most likely date for the founding of the church was A.D. 53-55, during Paul's Ephesian ministry (cf. Acts 19:10).[3]

---

[2] Frederick F. Bruce, "Colossians Problems, Part 1: Jews and Christians in the Lycus Valley," *Bibliotheca Sacra* 141 (1984): 6. *ATLA Religious Database*, EBSCOhost (21 November 2005).

[3] Curtis Vaughn, *Colossians and Philemon*, Bible Study Commentary (Grand Rapids, MI: Zondervan Publishing House), 1980. This writer accepts the Pauline authorship of Colossians, for he (Paul) resorted to describing the concept of reconciliation as the work of Christ on the cross in three other books that are generally accepted as his: Romans 5:9-11; 11:15; 2 Corinthians 5:16-21; and Ephesians 2:11-22 (see Derek Tidball, *The Message of the Cross* [Downers Grove, IL: InterVarsity Press, 2001], 217). Also, the opening and closing verses of Colossians affirm, and tradition accepts, that Paul wrote Colossians, though some have doubted, citing differences in vocabulary and the writing style from his other accepted books. Finally, the unbroken tradition of Pauline authorship, the close link with Philemon, which is assuredly Paul's, and the "thoroughly and characteristically Pauline theological background" outweigh literary hesitations for most scholars (see R. E. O. White, "Colossians," *The Broadman Bible Commentary*, vol. 11, ed. Clifton J. Allen [Nashville, TN: Broadman Press, 1971], 218. There are three dates offered as to when Paul wrote this letter: from imprisonment in Caesarea between A.D. 58-60; during his prison-period at Ephesus A.D. 5457; and/or during his Roman captivity between A.D. 61-63 (Acts 28:30). The latter date is the most widely-held view. So, Rome is the most likely location, and A.D. 61 is the most probable date, with recent hardships fresh in memory (Col 1:24) (see Patrick V. Rogers, "Colossians." *New Testament Message: A Biblical-Theological Commentary*, vol. 15, ed. Wilfrid Harrington and Donald Senior [Wilmington, DE: Michael Glazier, Inc., 1980], xixxx). Colossians

Introduction

There was a large Jewish population in the Lycus Valley, but the membership of the Colossian church was mainly Gentile (cf. 1:21, 27).[4] R. E. O. White adds as support Colossian 2:13 and perhaps Colossians 1:12. In a similar manner, White points out the implications of the scarcity of Old Testament allusions and the kind of vices named in 3:5-7. Only passing reference is made to the Jewish-Gentile controversy (3:11; 4:11).[5]

Finally, dangerous heresy was present in the Lycus Valley. At the time of this letter, it was a serious threat to the welfare of the Colossian church.[6] Francis W. Beare says that it is not altogether appropriate to call the system of religious teaching at this time "heresy" because the word could be used only by a kind of prolepsis. For until formal standards of orthodoxy have been established, there is no basis for defining any particular variety of teaching as heretical.[7] Most scholars consulted agree that there was a particular form of teaching

---

and Ephesians as companion epistles are very similar to each other in terms of historical background (see Vaughn, *Colossians and Philemon*, 15). In fact, Charles N. Pickell, *The Epistle to the Colossians: A Study Manual* (Grand Rapids, MI: Baker Book House Company, 1965), 15, cites Edgar Goodspeed as stating that three-fifths of Colossians is reflected in Ephesians. They both were written by Paul out of his prison experience and sent to believers in Asia Minor by Tychicus, the messenger who took them to their respective destination (cf. Col 4:7; Eph 6:21). Also, both cover many of the same topics. Even the language of the two epistles is very similar. Ephesians seems to be an expansion of ideas by Paul that he "presented in compact form in Colossians" (see Vaughn, *Colossians and Philemon*, 15). Bruce goes as far to say, "There would have been no letter to the Ephesians had there not first been a letter to the Colossians (see Bruce, "Colossians Problems, Part 4: Christ as Conqueror and Reconciler," 301).

4 Vaughn, *Colossians and Philemon*, 10.
5 White, 218.
6 Vaughn, *Colossians and Philemon*, 11.
7 Francis W. Beare and G. Preston MacLeod, "The Epistle to the Colossians," *The Interpreter's Bible*, vol. 11, ed. George A. Buttrick (Nashville, TN: Abingdon Press, 1955), 137.

current in the Lycus Valley, to which the church at Colossae and the neighboring churches were exposed. This teaching was on the surface attractive, but in reality its tendency was to undermine the gospel.[8] Bruce cites M. D. Hooker as questioning this position in a study she did in 1973. There she suggested that the data could be accounted for by Paul's arming his readers against the pressures of current society with its prevalent superstitions, just as "a Christian pastor in twentieth-century Britain might well feel it necessary to remind those in his care that Christ was greater than any astrological forces."[9] Bruce continues by indicating that the language points to a particular line of teaching against which the readers are put on guard and the most natural explanation for doing so would be that they were in some danger of being influenced by it.[10] Therefore, since most of what is said in the Colossian epistle is related in some way to this false teaching, it is imperative that one learns as much about it as he or she can.[11]

The error troubling Colossae clearly involved a form of syncretism which combined Jewish practice with pagan speculation.[12] Without doubt, Jewish elements are the stress upon Sabbaths, circumcision, the law, and probably the references to keeping festivals and new moon holy days (Col 2:11, 14,

---

[8] Frederick F. Bruce, "The Epistles to the Colossians, to Philemon, and to the Ephesians," *The New International Commentary on the New Testament*, vol. 10B (Grand Rapids, MI: William B. Eerdmans Publishing Company, 1984), 17.

[9] Bruce, "The Epistles to the Colossians, to Philemon, and to the Ephesians," 17-18.

[10] Bruce, "The Epistles to the Colossians, to Philemon, and to the Ephesians," 18.

[11] Vaughn, "Colossians and Philemon," 11.

[12] Geoffrey B. Wilson, *Colossians and Philemon* (Carlisle, PA: The Banner of Truth Trust, 1980), 11.

Introduction

16, 17). Colossians 3:11 and 4:11 also appear to presuppose a Judaist source of disagreement.[13] Vaughn cites Hort and Peake as stating that all of the diverse elements could be accounted for by Jewish teaching. On the other hand, pagan speculative elements undoubtedly included "philosophy" that depended upon credible methods of reasoning, which rested upon human tradition,[14] rather than upon the message of Christ and tending away from Him (Col 2:8). This, apparently, was not done by purposeful denial but as teaching a need of supplements to Christ and His work and other intermediations between the disciples and God (Col 2:18).[15] Lightfoot reasoned that the heresy was an incipient form of Gnosticism, reflecting modifications of the Jewish Essenes.[16]

There was a distinct asceticism, "with the appearance of wisdom in self-made religion and self-abasement and severe treatment of the body, but they are of no value against fleshly indulgence" (Col 2:23). This was possibly done to suppress the flesh and bring on visions (cf. Col 2:18), but this does not lead to a higher moral standard, and is "of no value against fleshly indulgence" (Col 2:23).[17]

Affirmation can also be made of the mediation of various principalities and powers (Col 1:16, 2:10, 2:15), elements of the world (Col 2:8, 2:20), and angels (Col 2:18), who were taken as spiritual powers that were involved in

---
13 Vaughn, *Colossians and Philemon*, 11.
14 White, 219.
15 H. C. G. Moule, *Studies in Colossians & Philemon* (Grand Rapids, MI: Kregel Publications, 1977), 31.
16 J. B. Lightfoot, *Saint Paul's Epistles to the Colossians and to Philemon* (Grand Rapids, MI: Zondervan Publishing House, 1879, 1961), 76-77, 82.
17 Roy Yates, *The Epistle to the Colossians* (London: Epworth Press, 1993), xiv.

the creation of the world, the work of redemption, and the whole process of delivery. The false teaching stressed that these strange powers, which stood between the believer and God, be placated and worshiped (Col 2:15, 18, 19) in order to aid the worshipper in ascending to the heavenly realm. As a result of this, Christ was consigned to a relatively inferior place in the Colossian schema.[18] H. C. G. Moule states, "One thing is certain as to the 'Colossian Heresy.' It was a doctrine of God, and of salvation, which cast a cloud over the glory of Jesus Christ."[19]

In the end, the Colossian error was to loosen a person's hold on the Christ they had first been taught (Col 2:19; cf. 2:6-7); indeed, to distort and even deny the uniqueness of the exalted Lord, the only mediator, through whom they had once been set free. Paul's answer, without doubt, is a Christology of cosmic magnitude. He strongly emphasized the fullness of deity dwelling in Christ; Christ's supremacy in creation over all things, including thrones or powers or rulers or authorities (Col 1:16); his headship over them in status (Col 2:10); his victory over them through the cross (Col 2:14, 15).[20] White concludes that Paul's position in the book of Colossians is: "To doubt the fullness of Christ is to miss the fullness, richness, and sufficiency of the Christian life."[21]

There are people today, as then, who love to show off their exceptional piety. They declare that they have reached a higher

---

18 Yates, xiv, in agreement with Vaughn, *Colossians and Philemon*, 11.
19 H. C. G. Moule, *Colossians and Philemon Studies* (Minneapolis, MN: Klock & Klock Christian Publishers, Inc., 1981), 9; quoted in Vaughn, *Colossians and Philemon*, 11.
20 White, 220.
21 White, 220.

level of spiritual experience, as though they had been initiated into sacred mysteries which give them a superior advantage over the uninitiated. Paul warns that their boasting of the special insight, which they have received from divine reality, are simply inflated by unspiritual pride and are out of touch with Him who is the true head and fount of life and knowledge.[22] They are still in need of the message of Colossians which emphasizes that believers are only complete in Christ's fullness, and that faith in him makes reliance upon any subordinate powers unnecessary, for nothing in all the universe is outside the scope of his sovereignty. The contemporary application of this teaching should not escape the Church's role in this type of ministry at a time when people everywhere are still held in bondage by forces they cannot control.[23]

CHRIST AS CONQUEROR

In his widely acclaimed book, *Christus Victor*, the Swedish theologian, Gustav Aulén, stated that the "dramatic" and "classic" idea of the Atonement is that of Christ's gaining the victory over evil. More specifically, he says, "Its central theme is the idea of the Atonement as a Divine conflict and victory; Christ—Christus Victor—fights against and triumphs over the evil powers of the world, the 'tyrants' under which mankind is in bondage and suffering, and in Him God reconciles the world to Himself."[24]

---

22 Frederick F. Bruce, "Colossian Problems, Part 3: The Colossian Heresy," *Bibliotheca Sacra* 141 (2004): 195-208. *ATLA Religious Database*, EBSCOhost (21 November 2005).
23 Wilson, 13.
24 Gustav Aulén, *Christus Victor: A Historical Study of the Three Main Types of the Idea of Atonement* (London: Society for Promoting Christian Knowledge, 1931; reprint, New York: MacMillan, 1967), 4.

Christ as Conqueror and Reconciler

Aulén further points out that the background of the view is dualistic,[25] that is, God is seen as in Christ carrying on a victorious conflict against powers of evil which are hostile to His will. Aulén continues by saying that this constitutes Atonement because the drama is cosmic in nature, and the victory over the hostile powers creates a new relationship—a relationship of reconciliation—between God and the world. Moreover, Aulén says, "Because in a measure the hostile powers are regarded as in the service of the Will of God the Judge of all, and the executants of His judgment. Seen from this side, the triumph over the opposing powers is regarded as a reconciling of God Himself; He is reconciled by the very act in which He reconciles the world to Himself."[26]

Tidball reiterates Aulén's idea when he points out that the focus of the "classic" view is on the work of Christ as a work of Atonement, not just of salvation.[27] In fact, Aulén says it more succinctly when he states:

> It is important, above all, at this point to see clearly that the work of salvation and deliverance is at the same time a work of atonement, of reconciliation between God and the world. It is altogether misleading to say that the triumph of Christ over the powers of evil, whereby He

---

[25] By which he explains that he uses Dualism in the sense in which the idea constantly occurs in Scripture, of the opposition between God and that which in His own created world resists His will, between the Divine Love and the rebellion of created wills against Him. This Dualism is an altogether radical opposition, but it is not an absolute Dualism; for in the scriptural view, evil has not an eternal existence. We shall see later that in the dominant theology of the eighteenth and nineteenth centuries, there was a tendency to confuse this scriptural idea of Dualism with the two other forms, and therefore, is an effort to escape from it and to minimize its importance (see Aulén, 5).

[26] Aulén, 5.

[27] Tidball, 248.

delivers man, is a work of salvation but not of atonement; for the two ideas cannot possibly be separated. It is precisely the work of salvation wherein Christ breaks the power of evil that *constitutes* the atonement between God and the world; for it is by it that He removes the enmity, takes away the judgment which rested on the human race, and reconciles the world to himself, not imputing their trespasses (2 Cor 5:18).[28]

In support of Aulén's idea that this is "the" New Testament interpretation of the cross, Tidball cites Aulén as drawing upon 1 Corinthians 15; 2 Corinthians 5:19; and Colossians 2:14. In continuing, Aulén also interprets the central atonement argument of Romans 4-7 and references Galatians 3:10-13, concerning the curse of the law; so he can present the law as an enemy, one of the hostile powers that Christ defeated.[29]

Tidball cites several theologians who have justifiably criticized Aulén's position. The first one he quotes is John McIntyre, who speaks for many when he says that "although this view of the atonement has a legitimate claim to be *one* of the New Testament models, the preeminence Aulén gives it is unwarranted, and 'it is a case of a brilliant idea being overstated.'"[30] Tidball, then, cites Colin Gunton, who fears that Aulén gains more from Origen than he does from the New Testament. Gunton also adds that Aulén presents the atonement as a cosmic drama similar to the mythical stories of gods at war, rather than as a real, earthly story in which a human Christ battles against temptation and continuously

---

28 Aulén, 71.
29 Tidball, 248.
30 Tidball, 248.

wins victories over the demonic.³¹ Gunton is further referenced as saying that the cross "is not so much a divine drama as a divine *and* human drama."³² Gunton concludes by noting that while the Bible certainly does use the metaphor of victory, "The language of victory does not then give us a theory, something final and fixed forever, but one way into the many-sided reality of the cross."³³

Tidball concludes the critiques of Aulén's position by acknowledging that even though Aulén's argument has not convinced many that it is the "classic" view of the atonement, it has been successful in resurrecting a neglected insight that does have some safe and sound basis in the New Testament.³⁴ Tidball continues by stressing that "throughout the New Testament, the cross is seen as a triumph, not as a defeat. It is spoken of with joyful confidence and in terms of victory."³⁵ That, of course, as John Stott notes is a matter of unexpectation, for "any contemporary observer, who saw Christ die, would have listened with astonished incredulity to the claim that the Crucified was a Conqueror."³⁶

CHRIST AS RECONCILER

Although the concept of Christ as being the agent in reconciliation is not widely mentioned in the New Testament or discussed by others in the immediate post-apostolic period, it is one of the most dominant interpretations of

---

31 Tidball, 248.
32 Tidball, 248.
33 Tidball, 248-249.
34 Tidball, 249
35 Tidball, 249.
36 Stott, 227.

the cross today.[37] Perhaps, it is "the most popular," writes John Stott ". . . because it is the most personal."[38] Unlike other concepts of bygone eras, "this one belongs to the contemporary world where people are searching for genuine relationships and struggling with the results of unsatisfactory ones."[39] This makes it more necessary to gain a fuller understanding of the cross of Christ from the standpoint of reconciliation.

From a biblical perspective, Bruce states that the idea is unique to Paul among New Testament writers. In continuing, Bruce says that Paul is the only writer to mention reconciliation in a theological sense.[40] In drawing from several sources, Tidball gives some cogent reasons as to why the concept of reconciliation is significant to Paul: First, there is the "mildly surprising" fact that only Paul among New Testament writers describes the cross as a work of reconciliation. Second, he seems to use language in an exceptional way when speaking of God's reconciling Himself to humankind. Finally, there is value, not just appeal, in explaining the cross as reconciliation itself. It is the least metaphorical and most concrete way of speaking of the new relationship between God and humankind that results from Christ's death.[41]

The idea leads in two directions at the same time. It leads into the heart of the Gospel, giving more specific information on how it was affected.[42] Frank Stagg, years earlier, used

---

37 Tidball, 218.
38 Stott, 192.
39 Tidball, 218.
40 Frederick F. Bruce, "Colossians Problems, Part 4: Christ as Conqueror and Reconciler," 291.
41 Tidball, 217.
42 Tidball, 217.

similar words in describing reconciliation. He said that "the *idea* of reconciliation goes to the heart of the New Testament doctrine of salvation."[43] Tidball expands the concept by saying that it also extends outwardly to the circumference of the Gospel, revealing more than any other metaphor of salvation about how it is to be applied. The way Paul develops the idea shows that it was more important to him, not just in terms of salvation, but also in relation to a range of experiences and duties in the Christian life.[44] In light of this, Tidball quotes Ralph Martin as claiming that reconciliation "can be presented as an interpretive key to Paul's theology; and if we are pressed to suggest a simple term that summarizes his message, the word reconciliation will be the 'chief theme' or 'centre' of his missionary and pastoral thought and practice."[45]

There is a sense of progression in Paul's development of the theme of reconciliation in his writings.[46] It is God "who reconciled us to Himself through Christ," he told the Church in Corinth (2 Cor 5:18). Paul reminds those in Rome: "We were reconciled to God through the death of His Son" (Rom 5:10). He speaks of himself and those to whom he writes as being entrusted with "the ministry of reconciliation" (2 Cor 5:18). Paul continues by saying that the Gospel which they preach is "the word of reconciliation" (2 Cor 5:19) because in it the invitation is given on behalf of Christ: "be reconciled to God" (2 Cor 5:20). Those who respond in faith to the invitation "have now received the reconciliation" (Rom 5:11); they "have peace

---

43 Stagg, 102.
44 Tidball, 217.
45 Tidball, 217.
46 Tidball, 217, 229.

  Introduction

with God through our Lord Jesus Christ" (Rom 5:1).⁴⁷ In
Ephesians, Paul extends the concept of peace to include the
relationship between believing Jews and Gentiles when he
says that in Himself [He] "might reconcile them both in one
body to God through the cross" (Eph 2:15-16).

When Paul says, "God was in Christ reconciling the
world to Himself" (2 Cor 5:19), he seems to envision a
wider reference than only believers being included in God's
reconciling work. Bruce points out that the adverbial phrase
"in Christ" modifies the periphrastic verb "was reconciling." He maintains that even though the instrumental ἐν is
used instead of διὰ to express agency, Christ is once more
declared to be the Agent in God's work of reconciliation.
Bruce further states that the κόσμος in this verse may be
the world of humanity (as in John 3:16-17; 12:47); or it
may have an even wider dimension, like the creation which,
according to Romans 8:21, "will be set free from its slavery
to corruption into the freedom of the glory of the children
of God." Comparable to Romans 11:15, where the "reconciliation of the world" (καταλλαγὴ κόσμου) is the sequel
to Israel's rejection, it suggests that it is the whole human
race that is indicated.⁴⁸

Finally, in this section on Christ as reconciler, Bruce indicates that the tense of the verb, translated "reconcile" in
2 Corinthians 5:19, is not aorist or perfect; it is periphrastic
imperfect (ἦν ... καταλλάσσων). This means that "the reconciliation of the κόσμος is a continuous process, not yet an

---
47 Bruce, "Colossians Problems, Part 4: Christ as Conqueror and Reconciler,"
291.
48 Bruce, "Colossians Problems, Part 4: Christ as Conqueror and Reconciler,"
292.

13

Christ as Conqueror and Reconciler

accomplished fact. Its completion, as Romans 11:15 indicates, lies in the future. When the reconciliation of believers is spoken of, it is indeed an accomplished fact: God who, in Christ, is in the process of 'reconciling the κόσμος to Himself' (2 Cor 5:19), has through that same Christ "reconciled us [believers] to Himself" (2 Cor 5:18).[49] To reiterate, the reconciliation of believers is a completed work, while the reconciliation of the world is a continuous process.[50]

RATIONALE FOR THE RESEARCH

There is a close relationship between the portrayals of Christ as Reconciler in the Christological hymn of Colossians 1:15-20 and as Conqueror in Colossians 2:8-15. There are several passages of scripture to support the connection of the two pericopes. First, there is the mentioning of possibly similar spiritual forces in 1:16 and 2:15. Second, the full measure of deity, with the genitive in Colossians 2:9, is expressed in the same sense as in 1:19.[51] Third, both Colossians 1:20 and 2:15 refer to the cross as the event for reconciliation and triumph. Finally, Bruce states that perhaps Paul left the verb "to reconcile" unchanged in the Christological hymn (Col 1:20) because he was about to make it clearer in Colossians 2:10, 14, and 15 where the reconciliation of the hostile powers involved their defeat.[52]

---

49 Bruce, "Colossians Problems, Part 4: Christ as Conqueror and Reconciler," 292.

50 Bruce, "Colossians Problems, Part 4: Christ as Conqueror and Reconciler," 292.

51 Fredrick William Danker, ed., *A Greek-English Lexicon of the New Testament and Other Christian Literature* (Chicago, IL: The University of Chicago Press, 2000), 829.

52 Bruce, "Colossians Problem, Part 4: Christ as Conqueror and Reconciler," 293.

Introduction

In terms of interpretation of these scriptures, many studies were found that treated Christ, the Reconciler, as a separate entity from His role as Conqueror, with no mentioning of deliverance. Some studies dealt with the ideas, for the most part, separately; but made little allusion to deliverance.[53] Other studies intertwined the two concepts, with allusions to deliverance, without much distinction between them.[54]

Finally, there were two studies that were found to be the closest to this study. The first one was done by Gregory A. Boyd, who discusses all three concepts— more from a theological perspective than from a detailed exegetical one.[55] The second study was written by Bruce, who emphasizes the exegetical and theological aspects, but places very little stress on deliverance.[56] In this study, the concepts of Christ as Reconciler and Conqueror will be discussed, separately and jointly, with emphasis on the theological implications for the Church's role in deliverance—cosmically and individually. This study aims to help fill this void in scholarship for the purpose of gospel ministry.

DEFINITION OF TERMS

In order to understand how certain terms that are germane to this study are used, it is necessary to define the following:

Deliverance—the Old Testament concept of deliverance embraces the themes of safety (*yesu'a, tesu'a*) and escape (*peleta*). In the New Testament, deliverance involves the

---
53 Tidball, 228-231, 247-261.
54 Aulén, 71.
55 Boyd, 238-268.
56 Bruce, "Colossians Problems, Part 4: Christ as Conqueror and Reconciler," 291-302.

idea of being released or liberated from some evil situation such as torture (Heb 11:35) or bondage (Luke 4:18). The concept of deliverance from sin and the works of the devil is emphasized by Paul more fully in passages such as Acts 16:31; Ephesians 2:8; and 1 Thessalonians 1:10.[57]

καταλλαγή —the root idea in Greek is change of attitude or relationship.[58] The term occurs frequently in the KJV of the Old Testament as the rendering of the Hebrew root *kaphar* but only once in the New Testament (Rom 5:11), where it means "reconciliation." The English word "atonement" is derived from the words "at-one-ment," to make two parties as one, to reconcile two parties one to another. It means essentially "reconciliation." In modern usage, it has come to have a more restricted meaning, namely, *the process* by which the obstacles to reconciliation are removed.

In current usage, the phrase "to atone for" means the undertaking of a course of action, which was designed to undo the consequences of a wrong act with a view to the restoration of the relationship by the wrong act. To speak more precisely, it means the work of Christ, culminating at Calvary.[59]

In the Pauline school, the atoning act of God through the blood of the cross (i.e., Jesus' vicarious self-offering) may be lauded as the event that gives peace, stability, and redemption to all creation (Col 1:15-20; Eph 1:7-10).[60]

---

57 Walter A. Elwell, ed., "Deliverance," *Evangelical Dictionary of Theology*, 2d ed. (Grand Rapids, MI: Baker House Company, 2001), 330.
58 Elwell, "καταλλαγή," 992.
59 Alan Richardson, ed., "Reconciliation," *A Dictionary of Christian Theology* (Philadelphia: The Westminster Press, 1969), 18.
60 Erwin Fahlbusch and Geoffrey William Bromiley, eds., *The Encyclopedia of Christianity*, vol. 1 (Grand Rapids, MI: William B. Eerdmans Publishing Co., 1999), 155.

Introduction

Salvation—since the cosmos itself is in bondage, depressed under evil forces, the essential content of the word "salvation" is that the world itself will be rescued, renewed, or set free. Salvation is a cosmic event affecting the whole of creation. It is not simply the overcoming of my rebellion and the forgiveness of my guilt, but salvation is liberation of the whole world process of which I am a small part.[61]

Salvation as deliverance—the entire story of Israel in the Old Testament is the history of God's activity in saving his chosen people from all their enemies, material, and spiritual. The nature of salvation of Christ is demonstrated through the cross and Passion by showing the reality of God's forgiveness, and the brutal cost of Christ who, though sinless, and though pronounced sinless by the highest secular court of the day, faced the penalty of the worst sinner in society—death by crucifixion.[62]

Spiritual forces—are probably both personal and impersonal forces that hold human souls in bondage. These forces Christ vanquished on the Cross. He has shown Himself to be their Master, and those who are united to Him by faith need not have any fear of them.[63]

SUMMARY

In this chapter, an introduction to the study was provided, followed by a statement of the problem and purposes of the study. Then, a discussion of the Colossian church and heresy found there as the conditions for interpreting the

---
61 Boyd, 267.
62 Richardson, "Salvation as Deliverance," 300-302.
63 Bruce, "Colossians Problem, Part 4: Christ as Conqueror and Reconciler," 299.

selected passages of Scripture were given. Next, a background was laid for understanding the framework of the problem, including the rationale for the research. Finally, the definition of terms used in this study was presented.

Part II

Chapter Two

The Fullness of God in Christ:
The Reconciler
(Colossians 1:19-20)

This chapter treats Colossians 1:19-20—the first of the two passages selected for this study—through a detailed exegetical and theological exposition under the following headings: The Fullness of Christ and Christ as Reconciler. To fully appreciate the exposition of the concept of Christ as Reconciler, which is found at the end of the great Christological hymn of Colossians 1:15-20, it is necessary to summarize the verses leading up to it. In the hymn, Christ is attested as being the agent of God in both creation and reconciliation. His agency in creation is also supported by other New Testament scriptures. It is included in the letter to the Colossians as emphasis for the defense that those who have direct access to God through Christ and are united with Him are forbidden to worship beings or forces—no matter how powerful—because they are part of the created order which Christ brought into existence.[64] More specifically, Paul portrays Christ as the Son and Image of God in the sense that the nature and being of

---
64 Bruce, "Colossians Problems, Part 4: Christ as Conqueror and Reconciler," 291.

Christ as Conqueror and Reconciler

God are perfectly revealed in Him (cf. John 1:18);[65] He is first-born of all creation, in terms of priority in time and over it in rank and dignity; He is the one by whom all things hold together; He is head of the Church; He is first-born from the dead in true resurrection life, that is, never to die again (cf. 1 Cor 15: 20); and He is pre-eminent in all things.[66]

From the assistance of several theologians, Weaver pulls together the essence of this portion of the hymn by stating that the appropriate understanding of creation means that it needs not be deified nor shunned, neither does it require one to fear it nor worship it. Creation must not become a power which controls and enslaves persons' lives. When Christ is recognized as the Lord of creation, this enables them to achieve the freedom to use it responsibly. People should not lament their humanness and choose ascetic withdrawal or rejection of the world. A universe created by, through, and for Christ is good; therefore, it cannot be dualistic. In fact, the hymn declares that matter and spirit were both involved in the divine act of creation (Col 1:16). Weaver concludes that the world "does more than exist because of Christ; it becomes the only place where humanity can find authentic existence under the gracious rule of the Lord who manifests the loving creator God."[67] In summarizing the hymn, thus far, as the context for understanding the last two verses, Eduard Schweitzer says it well in his perception of creation

---

65 Curtis Vaughn, "Colossians," *The Expositor's Bible Commentary*, vol. 11, ed. Frank E. Gaebelein (Grand Rapids, MI: Zondervan Publishing House, 1978), 181.
66 Rogers, xx.
67 James Albert Weaver, "Colossians 1:15-20 and Its Function in the Letter" (Ph.D. diss., The Southern Baptist Theological Seminary, School of Theology, 1982), 125-126, University Microfilms International, 5420 (1982).

The Fullness of God in Christ: The Reconciler

from a Christological perspective: "When we look at Jesus, we understand what real love and unselfishness is, and since our hymn says that the origin and the final goal of the whole creation is in Christ, it says that God can only be understood rightly if we understand him as the river of love that flows from the creation of the world through to its consummation."[68]

Having now established the preeminence of Christ in His being in the image of God, the Creator of the universe, and the head of the Church, Paul now reveals Christ's preeminence in terms of His redeeming work. The nature of this work is that of reconciliation.[69]

THE FULLNESS OF CHRIST: COLOSSIANS 1:19

19 ὅτι ἐν αὐτῷ εὐδόκησεν πᾶν τὸ πλήρωμα κατοικῆσαι[70]

19 For He (God) willed all the fullness to dwell in Him (Christ),[71] [or] For all the fullness was well pleased to dwell in Him (Christ)[.]

Before dealing further with the concept of reconciliation, it is necessary to look closer at the basis for Christ's supremacy. Christ is supreme because "[For] it was the Father's

---

68 Eduard Schweizer, "Christ in the Letter to the Colossians," *Review and Expositor* 70 (1973): 456-457; quoted in Weaver, 125.
69 Charles R. Erdman, *The Epistles of Paul to the Colossians and to Philemon* (Philadelphia: The Westminster Press, 1933), 50.
70 All Greek references are from *The Greek New Testament*, 4th ed. Revised (Stuttgart: United Bible Societies, 2001).
71 Unless otherwise noted the translations of Greek verses in this study are the author's.

good pleasure for all the fullness to dwell in Him" (Col 1:19, NASB). The subject of the verb translated "it was the good pleasure" is uncertain. Vaughn cites C. F. D. Moule as taking it as referring to Christ and Lightfoot as recognizing this view as being "grammatically possible," but thinks "it confuses the theology of the passage hopelessly."[72]

Others construe the subject to be "fullness."[73] In addition, Vaughn says that most interpreters understand the passage as assuring the action of God. The phrase means then that God willed that in Christ all fullness should reside.[74]

Vaughn cites Scott as saying that the word translated "fullness" is "perhaps the most difficult" in the epistle and is the focus of much discussion.[75] In addition, Vaughn points out that the term is found about seventeen times in the New Testament, but only four of those places are analogous to the present passage. They are Ephesians 1:23 ("the fullness of Him who fills all in all"); Ephesians 3:19 ("the fullness of God"); Ephesians 4:13 ("the fullness of Christ"); and Colossians 2:9 ("the fullness of Deity").[76]

The NIV understands the passage as affirming an action of God. God willed that in Christ all fullness should dwell, that is, as an ingressive aorist; it means to take up permanent abode.[77] Bruce, on the other hand, states that an explicit subject for the verb is offered in the clause itself:

---

72 Vaughn, *Colossians and Philemon*, 43-44.
73 Vaughn, *Colossians and Philemon*, 43-44.
74 Vaughn, *Colossians and Philemon*, 43-44.
75 Vaughn, *Colossians and Philemon*, 44.
76 Vaughn, *Colossians and Philemon*, 44.
77 Cleon L. Rogers, Jr., and Cleon L. Rogers, III, *The Linguistic and Exegetical Key to the Greek New Testament* (Grand Rapids, MI: Zondervan Publishing House, 1998), 461.

The Fullness of God in Christ: The Reconciler

"the fullness was well pleased to take up residence in Him" (as in the RSV: "in him all the fullness of God was pleased to dwell"). It cannot be decided with certainty whether ὁ θεὸς (understood) or πᾶν τὸ πλήρωμα (expressed) is the more probable subject. It is clear though as to Paul's intention; it is repeated more fully in Colossians 2:9: "For in Him [i.e., Christ] all the fullness of Deity dwells in bodily form."[78] Gaebelein says the same thing when he suggests that nothing of Deity is lacking in Christ. He adds that the similar expression found in Colossians 2:9 lends support to this view.[79] Danker agrees to as much when he writes that the full measure of Deity mentioned in 1:19, without the genitive, is also found in the same sense in 2:9.[80] Bruce concludes that if Colossians 1:19 is construed to mean that "in Him all fullness of deity was well pleased to take up residence," then, the double aorist, εὐδόκησεν and κατοικῆσαι are perhaps pointing to the time of His resurrection or exaltation. This is in effect the same as saying that God Himself, in all His fullness, was pleased to dwell in Him. No essential difference exists in the meaning of the two constructions.[81]

The word for "fullness" seems to have been in current use by the false teachers and was possibly, though not certainly, employed by them of the totality of supernatural powers

---

78 Frederick F. Bruce, "Colossian Problems, Part 2: The 'Christ Hymn' of Colossians 1:15-20," *Bibliotheca Sacra* 141 (1984): 99-111. ATLA Religious Database, EBSCOhost (21 November 2005), 107.
79 Vaughn, "Colossians," 185.
80 Danker, 829.
81 Bruce, "Colossians Problems, Part 2: "The 'Christ Hymn' of Colossians," 107-108.

("aeons") that they believed were in control of men's lives.[82] Bruce also concedes that the term may have been used that way here, but cautions that nothing can be established on the bare ground of its being a possibility.[83]

It is significant that Paul says "all" the fullness dwells in Christ. The Colossian errorists perhaps looked upon the many spirit beings as filling the space between God and the world as intermediaries and taught that any communication between God and the world has to pass through them. They probably included Christ among these supernatural powers, admitting that He was of heavenly origin and that God was in some sense present in Him. Paul, on the other hand, declares that Christ is not just one of many divine beings; He is the one and only Mediator between God and the world. Therefore, all of the attributes and actions of God are centered in Him.[84]

Vaughn gives this as a second reason for ascribing universal supremacy to Christ in His work of reconciliation. The Father was pleased through Him (Christ) to reconcile all things to Himself (v. 20, ASV). The statement shows a close connection to verse 19. In fact, the Greek word for "to reconcile" (v. 20) is parallel to the Greek word for "dwell" (v. 19), both terms being grammatically reliant on the verb rendered: "it was the good pleasure" (v. 9, ASV). The Father willed that all fullness should dwell in Christ; He also willed to reconcile all things to Himself through Christ. Also, another factor showing the intimate connection between verses 19 and 20 is that the action declared in verse 20 is

---

82 Vaughn, "Colossians," 185.
83 Bruce, "Colossians Problems, Part 2: "The 'Christ Hymn' of Colossians," 108.
84 Vaughn, "Colossians," 185-186.

The Fullness of God in Christ: The Reconciler

dependent upon that of verse 19. Only one in whom the divine fullness dwelled could bring about reconciliation.[85] To conclude this section on the exposition of verse 19 and then transition to verse 20, Bruce's words seem appropriate: "It was God's good pleasure, moreover, to 'reconcile all things to Himself' through Christ. The fullness of divine energy is manifested in Him in the work of reconciliation as well as in that of creation. In the words that follow in Colossians 1 this reconciling activity is applied particularly to redeemed humanity, but first its universal aspect comes into view. In reconciliation as in creation the work of Christ has a cosmic significance; it is God's eternal purpose (as stated in Eph. [sic] 1:10) that all things should be summed up in Him."[86]

CHRIST AS RECONCILER: COLOSSIANS 1:20

20 καὶ δι' αὐτοῦ ἀποκαταλλάξαι τὰ πάντα εἰς αὐτόν, εἰρηνοποιήσας διὰ τοῦ αἵματος τοῦ σταυροῦ αὐτοῦ, [δι' αὐτοῦ] εἴτε τὰ ἐπὶ τῆς γῆς εἴτε τὰ ἐν τοῖς οὐρανοῖς.[87]

---

85 Vaughn, 185-186.
86 Bruce, Colossian Problems, Part 2: "The 'Christ Hymn' of Colossians 1:15-20," 109.
87 There is textual problem in the last part of verse 20 in the phrase, δι' αὐτοῦ, where it is either retained or omitted from the text altogether. Based upon the witnesses and dates, this writer believes that the support is weak for omitting the phrase. The strength of the external evidence for retaining the phrase is based upon the number and quality of the text type, the wide geographical distribution of the text type, the range of dates, and the roughness of the reading. In terms of internal evidence, a strong case can be made for retaining the phrase because it conforms to the style and vocabulary of the rest of the passage. Note verse 16, where it is clear from the beginning of the verse that all things were created by Him (Christ). At the end of the same verse, Paul restates it again. He seems to use this method of restating for emphasis—maybe even to drive the point home to the Gnostics that Christ really is supreme (see Bruce M. Metzger, *A Textual Commentary on the Greek New Testament* [New York: United Bible Societies,

Christ as Conqueror and Reconciler

20 And by having made peace through the blood of His cross, by Him to reconcile all things unto Himself; by Him, whether the things upon the earth or the things in the heavens.

Tidball points out that this is the final reference in Paul's writings to reconciliation, which includes Colossians 1:21-23, where similar familiar material to that discussed in chapter one is found. The same emphasis is found on the estrangement of humanity from God, the initiative of God in reconciliation, the agency of Christ, and humankind's need to receive reconciliation through faith.[88]

When one turns to Colossians 1:19-20, new aspects of the work of reconciliation are found. The statement at the end of the hymn is that God, who was well pleased in all His fullness to dwell in Christ, was pleased also "through Him to reconcile all things to Himself, having made peace through the blood of His cross; through Him, *I say,* whether things on earth or things in heaven" (Col 1:20, NASB). Two developments in Paul's writing take place in this verse. First, he uses the compound verb ἀποκαταλλάσσω to translate "reconcile," instead of the usual καταλλάσσω. Tidball understands the word as possibly Paul's own creation used to intensify the focus on God's work of reconciliation.[89]

1971], 621; see also Bruce M. Metzger, *The Text of the New Testament* [New York: Oxford University Press, 1968], 207, 209-210; see M. Robert Mansfield, "Textual Criticism: Criteria for Evaluating Variants," class notes from GBIB 581, New Testament Hermeneutics and Exegesis, Oral Roberts University, fall 2004; see also M. Robert Mansfield, "Class Study Guide: New Testament Hermeneutics and Exegesis," class notes from GBIB 581, New Testament Hermeneutics and Exegesis, Oral Roberts University, fall 2004).
88 Tidball, 228.
89 Tidball, 229.

The Fullness of God in Christ: The Reconciler

Bruce would allow for the possibility of Paul's own creation but thinks too much should not be made of the compound verb here. For he points out that the same compound verb is used of the reconciliation of believers to God in Colossians 1:22 and the reconciliation of believing Jews and Gentiles in one body in Ephesians 2:16.[90] Tidball observes that only in this verse does Paul write about the cross reconciling *all things* as something different from reconciling repentant and believing sinners. It is a fact that Paul had written in 2 Corinthians 5:19 concerning God's reconciling "the world" (κόσμος) in Christ. It is clear there that Paul means the world of sinful humanity, and he does not have a wider category in mind; but here in verse 20, he writes in a non-personal way of "all things."[91]

Concerning the understanding of reconciliation in this verse, Tidball reports that scholars are in one of three groups. Some scholars attach the phrase closely to the verses that follow and state that the weight of the verse is on reconciliation that has been provided for the world but is only realized by those who have faith and believe the message Paul has spoken. If this is correct, Paul is not saying anything different from what he has said in his other writings. This position does not seem to be fair to the assertion that comes as the high point in his hymn of praise to Christ (Col 1:15-20), in which Christ's work is viewed from the standpoint of the creation and the new creation.[92]

Others broaden the scope of reconciliation but inter-

---
90 Bruce, "Colossians Problems, Part 4: "Christ as Conqueror and Reconciler," 292.
91 Tidball, 229.
92 Tidball, 229.

pret the "all things" to include the world of angels, rulers, powers, and authorities with which the book of Colossians is very much concerned but is mentioned specifically in verse 2:15. Although they no doubt are included, there seems to be no reason to limit Paul's claim like this.[93]

The most natural interpretation, given the context, is that "all things" speaks of the whole universe. The term takes for granted that the whole world has experienced a substantial disruption in its relationship with God and is now functioning, in all aspects, in a state of alienation from Him. The death of Christ has changed all that and has made it possible for the universe to be restored in peace with God and to be brought once again to a state of order under His control. The explanation of how Christ's death accomplished such reconciliation is postponed until verse 2:15.[94] Tidball quotes O'Brien as saying that the important point, established here, is this: "Paul affirms that this universal reconciliation has been brought about, not in some otherworldly drama, but through something done in history, the death of Jesus on the cross."[95] His claim here is analogous to, but not exactly the same as, his understanding of "the future liberation of creation to be brought about when the children of God are finally revealed, which he mentions in Romans 8:19-21."[96] The result of this reconciliation is applied specifically to redeemed humanity, but first its universal aspect must be emphasized. As in creation, the reconciliation of Christ has cosmic importance; it is God's eternal purpose that all things should be summed up in

---

93 Tidball, 229.
94 Tidball, 229-230.
95 Tidball, 229.
96 Tidball, 230.

––––––– The Fullness of God in Christ: The Reconciler

Him (cf. Eph 1:10).[97] Vincent Taylor allows for the possible universality of Christ's reconciling work but understands reconciliation to be primarily the restoration of men to fellowship with God.[98] This is also the position of Ralph P. Martin, who states that "reconciliation is primarily concerned with the restoration of relationships."[99] He further points out that Paul persistently shows that speculative interest is not sufficient to match a moral problem. Martin recognizes the universal scope of Paul's teaching but states that the rationale for understanding the way in which the evil powers were overcome and forced to surrender their claim on Christ and His people is not given until Colossians 2:14-15. At this point in the text, Paul's teaching is primarily in the realm "of the personal effect of reconciliation by which its moral power is known, in the restoration to the favour (sic) of God [and] of men and women who formerly were estranged and hostile in mind and open transgressors (v. 21)."[100]

Boyd understands the need for reconciliation to be primarily for the "thrones," "dominions," "rulers," and "powers" that Christ created, but they have now apparently used their freedom to fight against His lordship rather than to carry out their functions in accord with it.[101] Bruce, on the

---

97 Bruce, "Colossians Problems, Part 2: The 'Christ Hymn' of Colossians 1:15-20," 109.
98 Vincent Taylor, *Forgiveness and Reconciliation: A Study in New Testament Theology* (London: Macmillan and Company, Limited, 1946), 79-84.
99 Ralph P. Martin, "Reconciliation and Forgiveness in Colossians," *Reconciliation and Hope: New Testament Essays on Atonement and Eschatology*, ed. Robert Banks (Grand Rapids, MI: William B. Eerdmans Publishing Company, 1974), 113.
100 Martin, "Reconciliation and Forgiveness in Colossians," 113-114.
101 Boyd, 247.

other hand, is more inclusive when he points out that if "all things," both in heaven and on earth, were created through Him, and yet, "all things," whether on earth or in heaven, are reconciled to God through Him, then it is logical that all things have been estranged from God their Creator.[102] Bruce concludes that everything in the universe has been subjected to Christ even as everything was created by and for Him.[103]

Boyd says that it is not obvious that "reconciliation," as Paul uses it in Colossians 1:20, and "redemption," as he and other New Testament writers use it elsewhere, are comparable ideas.[104] Boyd maintains, "It may be that in saying all things shall be ultimately reconciled to the lordship of Christ, Paul is simply saying that nothing will ultimately be able to effectively oppose this lordship. There is 'peace' throughout Christ's cosmos because everything is put in its proper place. In the case of the unredeemable hostile powers of darkness, this place is under Christ's feet."[105] Conversely, Bruce has no difficulty in accepting the two ideas as equivalent. He explains that the peace effected by the death of Christ may be freely accepted, or it may be imposed. He says that the reconciliation of the universe spoken of here includes what is now known as *pacification*. The principalities and powers whose defeat is presented in Colossians 2:15 are surely not portrayed as gladly conceding to divine grace

---

102 Bruce, "Colossians Problems, Part 2: The 'Christ Hymn' of Colossians 1:15-20," 109.
103 Bruce, "Colossians Problems, Part 2: The 'Christ Hymn' of Colossians 1:15-20," 109-110. Please note that the "universal" discussed above is not the same as "universalism," which denies the deity of Christ and teaches that everyone will be saved (see Frank Stagg, *The Holy Spirit Today* [Nashville, TN: Broadman Press, 1973], 15.)
104 Boyd, 248.
105 Boyd, 248-249.

The Fullness of God in Christ: The Reconciler

but as being forced to submit to a power greater than their own,[106] which is brought about by conquest.[107] Stott points out that this is very similar to what is described elsewhere in Paul's writings as: every knee bowing to Jesus and confessing his lordship (Phil 2:9-11), and all things being put under His feet by God, "until the day when they are brought together 'under one head, even Christ'" (Eph 1:10, 22).[108]

The essence of this chapter can be summed up as follows: Christ is able to reconcile all things to Himself because He is who He is; that is, God's fullness dwells in Him and works through Him.

---

106 Bruce, "Colossian Problems, Part 2: The 'Christ Hymn' of Colossians 1:15-20," 109.
107 Bruce, "Colossian Problems, Part 2: Christ as Conqueror and Reconciler," 293.
108 John R. Stott, *The Cross of Christ* (Downers Grove, IL: InterVarsity Press, 1986), 196.

Chapter Three

The Fullness of God in Christ:
The Forgiver and Conqueror
(Colossians 2:13-15)

Chapter three examines Colossians 2:13-15—the second of the two passages chosen for this study—with thorough exegesis and theological reflection under the following headings: Christ as Forgiver and Christ as Conqueror. There is a close relationship between the portrayal of Christ as Reconciler in Colossians 1:19-20 and His depiction as Conqueror in Colossians 2:13-15. Perhaps that was the reason that Paul left the verb "to reconcile" unchanged in 1:20, because he was about to make it clear in 2:13-15, where the reconciliation of the hostile powers involved their defeat.[109] Stott points out that, perchance, the most important New Testament passage in which the victory of Christ is set forth is Colossians 2:13-15.[110] Leivestad makes a similar statement concerning Colossians 2:14-15 when he says,

---

109 Bruce, "Colossian Problem, Part 4: Christ as Conqueror and Reconciler," 293.
110 Stott, 232-233.

"No other passage in Paul provides a stronger expression of the dramatic triumph of the crucified."[111]

In order to gain a fuller understanding of Colossians 2:13-15, it is necessary to give a summary of the larger context (2:8-15) in which it is found. In this larger context, Gaebelein states that Paul makes his most unswerving assail against the "the Colossian heresy."[112] He further points out that the tone of the passage is both admonitory and affirmative, but admonition is the dominant note sounded throughout. The affirmations, which primarily deal with Christ and His sufficiency (cf. vv. 9-15), form the foundation on which the warnings are issued and give point and power to them.[113]

Martin adds that 2:13-15 forms a condensed section in which the apostle is applying acts of God to his readers' circumstance. One major act was God's designation of His Son as "head of all rule and authority" (2:10), that is, the elemental spirits of the universe. The headship of Christ supports the original sense of 1:18a. In addition, there are scholars who see in this short passage, especially verses 14 and 15, a fragment of a hymn which celebrates the redeeming and victorious power of God in Christ.[114] Martin points out that there is a change in thought in verse 13. Starting with verse 10, where Christ is Lord of all the powers, Paul, then, discusses various ways in which the readers "have been made complete" (v. 10, NASB). Martin further shows that there are three phases in

---

111 Ragnar Leivestad, *Christ the Conqueror: Ideas of Conflict and Victory in the New Testament* (New York: The Macmillan Company, 1954), 100.
112 Vaughn, "Colossians," 197.
113 Vaughn, "Colossians," 197.
114 Martin, "Reconciliation and Forgiveness in Colossian," 116.

— The Fullness of God in Christ: The Forgiver and Conqueror

the initiation of that process: circumcision, baptism, and new life in the resurrection.[115] The depiction of Christ as Conqueror is presented in Colossians 2:15, which is the culmination of a passage which shows what God has done for His universe, including His people, in and through Christ.[116] Bruce further states that "the victory, like the creation and the reconciliation, is the work of God in Christ."[117] Stott points out that Paul in Colossians 2:13-15 puts together two diverse views of the saving work of Christ's cross. They are the forgiveness of sins and the cosmic overthrow of the principalities and powers.[118]

CHRIST AS FORGIVER: COLOSSIANS 2:13

13 καὶ ὑμᾶς νεκροὺς ὄντας [ἐν] τοῖς παραπτώμασιν καὶ τῇ ἀκροβυστίᾳ τῆς σαρκὸς ὑμῶν, συνεζωοποίησεν ὑμᾶς σὺν αὐτῷ, χαρισάμενος ἡμῖν πάντα τὰ παραπτώματα,[119]

---

115 Martin, "Reconciliation and Forgiveness in Colossians," 116.
116 Bruce, "Colossians Problems, Part 4: Christ as Conqueror and Reconciler," 293.
117 Bruce, "Colossians Problems, Part 4: Christ as Conqueror and Reconciler," 294.
118 Stott, 233.
119 There are two textual problems in verse 13. The first problem is whether there should be a change of personal pronouns in the middle part of the verse from the accepted reading ὑμᾶς to the unaccepted ἡμᾶς. The second problem is whether there should be a change of personal pronouns in the latter part of the verse from the accepted reading ἡμῖν to the unaccepted ὑμῖν. Based upon the witnesses and dates, this writer agrees that the accepted readings have the strongest support. The strength of the external evidence for retaining the accepted readings is based upon the number and quality of the text type, the wide geographical distribution of the text type, the range of the dates, and the roughness of the reading. Concerning the internal evidence for retaining ὑμᾶς, it is repeated for emphasis (see Metzger, *The Text of the New Testament*, 207, 209-210; see also Mansfield, "Textual Criticism: Criteria

Christ as Conqueror and Reconciler

13 Though you who were dead in your transgressions and the uncircumcision of your flesh, He (God) has made you alive together with Him (Christ), having forgiven us all our transgressions,

In addressing the Colossians in verse 13, Paul says, "And you." This is an emphatic position,[120] in which they were lacking in their innate ability to develop the principle necessary to overcome their sinful state and being devoid of spiritual circumcision and not separated from the guilt of sin nor from its power.[121] Clearly, "the uncircumcision" is used here in simply a figurative sense. He quickened you (or made you alive) together with him is a first aorist, active indicative of the double compound verb συζωοποιέω, to make alive (from ζάω contracted to ζώ and ποιέω) with σύν and repeated also with αὐτῷ (associative instrumental). It is found only here and in Ephesians 2:5, and apparently was fabricated by Paul for this passage. Most likely θεός (God) is the subject because He is clearly the subject in Ephesians 2:4f, and it is demanded by σὺν αὐτῷ here, referring to Christ. This can be correct even if Christ is the subject of ἦρκεν in verse 14. *Having forgiven us* is a first aorist, middle participle of χαρίζομαι, a common verb from χάρις. The act of forgiving is concurrent with being made alive, though logically before it.[122]

---

for Evaluating Variants"). In terms of internal evidence for ἡμῖν, the apostle at the earliest moment included "himself, claiming his share in the transgression and in the forgiveness. Paul used such transitions often (cf. 1:10-13, 3:3, 4; Eph 2: 2, 3, 13, 14, 4: 2, 31, 32); T. K. Abbot, *A Critical and Exegetical Commentary on the Epistles to the Ephesians and the Colossians: The International Critical Commentary*, vol. 36 (New York: Charles Scribner's Sons, 1897), 253-254.
120 A. T. Robertson, *Word Pictures in the New Testament*, vol. 4 (Nashville, TN: Broadman Press, 1930), 493.
121 H. C. G. Moule, "Studies in Colossians and Philemon," 105-106.
122 Robertson, 493-494.

— The Fullness of God in Christ: The Forgiver and Conqueror

Paul now shows how God was able to forgive, that is, to give graciously or forgive them out of grace,[123] of all their transgressions by quickening their faith in the risen Christ.[124] As Gentiles, Wilson points out that the Colossians had been doubly dead "through trespasses" and the "uncircumcision" of their flesh. They were cut off from the life of God by both their sins and their physical condition (cf. Eph 2:11-12). The latter was the true symbol of their unprivileged state as those who were far away from God's covenant mercy.[125]

As Paul comes to the heart of Christian experience, he includes himself with all believers by using "us."[126] Wilson cites J. B. Lightfoot as saying that Paul is "eager to claim his share in the transgression, that he may claim it also in the forgiveness."[127]

CHRIST AS CONQUEROR: COLOSSIANS 2:14

14 ἐξαλείψας τὸ καθ' ἡμῶν χειρόγραφον τοῖς δόγμασιν ὃ ἦν ὑπεναντίον ἡμῖν, καὶ αὐτὸ ἦρκεν ἐκ τοῦ μέσου προσηλώσας αὐτὸ τῷ σταυρῷ·

14 having cancelled the record of debts with the decrees which stood against us; and He has taken it from the center, by having nailed it to the cross.

---

123 Fritz Rienecker, "Colossians," in *A Linguistic Key to the Greek New Testament*, vol. 2, ed. Cleon L. Rogers, Jr. (Grand Rapids, MI: Zondervan Publishing House, 1980), 228.
124 H. C. G. Moule, "Studies in Colossians and Philemon," 106.
125 Wilson, 55.
126 Wilson, 55.
127 Wilson, 55.

Christ as Conqueror and Reconciler

Robert G. Bratcher and Eugene A. Nida say that Paul shows that the act of forgiveness of sins is similar to the cancellation of a record of debts.[128] In building from the idea of the forgiveness of sins, Bratcher and Nida state that the word for "cancelled" is the Greek verb for "wipe out," "erase." They further point out that the analogous Hebrew verb in the Old Testament is frequently used with *sin(s)* as the object (cf. Ps 51:9, 109:14; Isa 43:25; John 1:29; 1 John 3:5). Finally, they say that in order to express the concept of "cancelled," it is possible to use words such as "to tear up," "to throw away," or "to declare that it is no longer valid."[129] Wilson adds that "having forgiven" and "having blotted out" are both aorist participles. The first aorist participle shows that forgiveness was contemporaneous with God's quickening grace in conversion, while the second one names specifically the event by which this all inclusive pardon was secured (v. 14).[130] Randolph O. Yeager points out that the Greek word, χειρόγραφον, translated as "record of debt" or "bond," is a combination of χείρ and γράφω, which means something written by hand. It is a legal certificate that involves the "signer in legal obligations, such as a promissory note or contract which imposes upon the signer the payment of money or the performance of certain specified functions."[131] It is an IOU (that is, "I owe you").[132] Bratcher and Nida add that the record of our debt may be

---

128 Robert G. Bratcher and Eugene A. Nida. *A Handbook on Paul's Letters to the Colossians and to Philemon* (New York: United Bible Societies, 1977), 60, 61.
129 Bratcher and Nida, 60.
130 Wilson, 55.
131 Randolph O. Yeager, *The Renaissance New Testament*, vol. 15 (Gretna, LA: Pelican Publishing Company, 1998), 64.
132 Bratcher and Nida, 60.

The Fullness of God in Christ: The Forgiver and Conqueror

rendered as "the paper that says how much we owe," or "the list of all that we owe," or the "page that tells how many are our debts."[133] Undoubtedly, "the handwriting in decrees" was against the Jews, for they accepted it, but the Gentiles also gave moral consent to God's law, written in their hearts (Rom 2:14-15). Therefore, Paul affirms that the decrees "stood against us" because neither the Jews nor Gentiles could keep it. It is arresting that Paul connected the common word χειρόγραφον for "bond" or "debt" with the cross of Christ. In addition, Robertson affirms, "And he has taken it out of the way." This is a perfect, indicative of αἴρω, which is an old, common verb that means "to lift up," "to bear," "to take away."[134] Robertson further points out that the perfect tense stresses the permanence of the removal of the bond, which has been compensated and cancelled and cannot be offered again. God has taken the bond that was against us "out of the midst," from between us and God, as a barrier to our peace, and nailed it to the cross. This is a first aorist, active participle of an old, common verb, which means to fasten with nails to a thing.[135] Moule comments that there appears to be no support for the so-called practice of canceling a bond by piercing it with a nail.[136] Nor does the image here seem to refer to the cancellation of a bond by marking it out with an X, that is, crossing it out. The expression "nailing it to the cross"

---
133 Bratcher and Nida, 60.
134 Robertson, 494, in agreement with Wilson, 55-56.
135 Robertson, 494-495, in agreement with C. F. D. Moule, *The Epistles of Paul the Apostle to the Colossians and to Philemon*, Cambridge Greek Testament Commentary, ed. C. F. D. Moule (Cambridge: The Cambridge University Press, 1958), 107.
136 C. F. D. Moule, *The Epistles of Paul the Apostle to the Colossians and to Philemon*, 99.

may mean "attaching the record to the cross with a nail" or "using a nail to put the record on the cross." Since the expression is basically metaphorical, it may be necessary, as in other places, to mark the symbolic usage by means of an expression that indicates similarity or likeness; for example, "nailing it, so to speak, to the cross" or "as it were, nailing it to the cross."[137]

Bratcher and Nida add that the pronoun "it" has reference here to the record of one's debts, but it may seem rather peculiar to talk about doing away with a record by "nailing it to the cross." The idea is not that the record was eliminated in the process, but that it was made no longer legitimate in the sense that the death of Christ on the cross wiped out one's sense of obligation. Thus, the phrase "did away with it" may be articulated as "made it ineffective" or "caused it no longer to have power" or even "destroyed its meaning."[138]

Robertson says because Christ took the record of one's debts to the cross, the victim was also nailed to the cross with Him when God nailed the law to His cross. Therefore, the "bond" is cancelled for humankind.[139] Leivestad points out that this means that God cancels the debts, but He also abolishes the law on which it was based, for the requirements of the law form the basis of the charge against humankind. Thus, both the bond and the law are against us.[140] Leivestad further states that τοῖς δόγμασιν must be understood in accordance with verse 20 and Ephesians 2:14, which refer to a vivid and metaphorical expression of the Mosaic law.

---
137 Bratcher and Nida, 61
138 Bratcher and Nida, 61.
139 Robertson, 494-495.
140 Leivestad, 102, in agreement with Wilson, 55-56.

— The Fullness of God in Christ: The Forgiver and Conqueror

Leivestad concedes that the identification of χειρόγραφον with all of the Mosaic law is not necessarily implied, but it represents in any case the debt which humans have incurred for themselves through their trespasses against the law.[141] Pickell adds that humans are required to obey God's law, and, failing to do so, it is scored against them. He continues by saying that Christ removed their guilt and bore it on the cross. It is even better that "the record is blotted out so that not a trace remains (cf. Gal 3:13; 2 Cor 5:21)."[142] Leivestad declares what really happened the instant the hostile powers thought they were being victorious, nailing Christ to the cross, was that God also nailed humankind's charge to the cross, disarmed the powers, and triumphed over them in the Crucified One.[143] Christ became the end of the law the second He yielded to the verdict of the law. The idea of the vicarious punishment of Jesus appears to be assumed.[144]

Stott says much the same thing that other authors have said, but argues that "the written code, with its regulations, that was against us" can hardly be a reference to the law in itself, since Paul regarded it as "holy, and the commandment is holy and righteous and good" (Rom 7:12, NASB); it must rather refer to the broken law, which on that account was "against us and stood opposed to us" with its verdict.[145]

Moule makes a distinction between the "revelatory" sense of "Law" in the writings of Paul and its legalistic sense,

---
141 Leivestad, 102.
142 Pickell, 50, in agreement with Wilson, 55-56.
143 Leivestad, 102.
144 Leivestad, 102.
145 Joachim Jeremias, *Central Message of the New Testament* (London: SCM Press, 1966), 37; quoted in Stott, 233-234.

and he uses this difference to offer an acceptable answer to the question as to whether Christ abolished the Law or not. "Paul," Moule says, "saw Christ as the *fulfillment* of the law, when law means God's revelation of Himself and of His character and purpose; but as the *condemnation* and *termination* of any attempt to use law to justify oneself."[146] Bruce contends that those who undertook to observe the Law either as a means of getting right with God or as the way to higher attainment in spiritual experience soon found that the Law, instead of helping them, bore witness against them.[147]

In continuing, Bruce states that probably the first commentary on these words in Colossians is Paul's explanation in Ephesians 2:15 where Christ has abolished "in His flesh . . . the Law of commandments contained in ordinances." Bruce says that Paul was writing there concerning the removal of the barrier that in the past separated Jews from Gentiles. By saying that "Christ abolished . . . the Law of commandments," Paul goes as far as anything that he says in Galatians 3:19-4:4 or 2 Corinthians 3:7-16. Bruce concludes that the verb "'abolish' (καταργέω) is not used of annulment of the old order in Galatians as it is in 2 Corinthians and Ephesians, but the same idea is expressed in other words. And if it be asked how these plainspoken statements can be squared with Romans 3:31—where Paul says that through faith we do not 'abolish' (καταργέω) the Law but

---

[146] C. F. D. Moule, "Obligation in the Ethic of Paul," *Christian History and Interpretation*, ed. W. R. Farmer, C. F. D. Moule, and R. R. Niebuhr (New York: Cambridge University Press, 1967), 392; quoted in Bruce, "Colossians Problems, Part 4: Christ as Conqueror and Reconciler," 295.

[147] Bruce, "Colossians Problems, Part 4: Christ as Conqueror and Reconciler," 295.

rather establish it—the answer can only be that in Romans 3:31 'Law' bears its revelatory sense."[148]

In dealing with the matter of the subject(s) of the verbs in verses 13-15, Bratcher and Nida state that in Greek, "God" is clearly the subject of the verb in verse 13: "He made you alive (with Him)," and thereafter, there is no name or pronoun to identify the subject of the remaining verbs. Most translations and commentaries examined take "God" as the subject of all the verbs in verses 13-15. Bratcher and Nida cite Wey as seeming to make "Christ" the subject of all the verbs. They portray Moule as making a change of subject, occurring with the first participle "having cancelled" (RSV) in verse 14. Bratcher and Nida point out that Lightfoot understands the change of subject at the words in verse 14: "he set aside" (RSV).[149] Several versions (TEV, SpCL, and BrCL) make the change in verse 15 with Christ as the subject of the verbs.[150] Bratcher and Nida also understand the "subject of the verbs—two participles, one before and one after the main verb—as continuing to be God from verse 13."[151] Bruce agrees with Bratcher and Nida's position but adds that such a change of subject might be possible if verses 14 and 15 contain the quotation of a hymn, celebrating in graphic language the redemption accomplished by Christ on the cross, but that remains hypothetical.[152]

---

148 Bruce, "Colossians Problems, Part 4: Christ as Conqueror and Reconciler," 295-296.
149 Bratcher and Nida, 61.
150 Bratcher and Nida, 61.
151 Bratcher and Nida, 61, in agreement with Robertson, 495.
152 Bruce, "Colossians Problems, Part 4: Christ as Conqueror and Reconciler," 294.

CHRIST AS CONQUEROR: COLOSSIANS 2:15

15 ἀπεκδυσάμενος τὰς ἀρχὰς καὶ τὰς ἐξουσίας ἐδειγμάτισεν ἐν παρρησίᾳ, θριαμβεύσας αὐτοὺς ἐν αὐτῷ.

15 He has disarmed the rulers and the authorities, and has made a public example (of them), having triumphed over them by it (the cross) or in Him (Christ).

Paul moves further from the forgiveness of sins to the conquest of the evil powers.[153] Stott states that it is significant that Paul reinforces with parallel phrases what Christ did to the χειρόγραφον, canceling and removing it, with what He did to the principalities and powers, disarming and conquering them;[154] and He does this by using three graphic verbs to portray their defeat. The first could mean that God in Christ "stripped" them from self like foul clothing because they had closed in upon Him and were clinging to Him, and so He "discarded" them (NEB). A better interpretation is that He "stripped" them either of their weapons and so "disarmed" them (NIV) or of "their dignity and might" and so degraded them.[155]

Leivestad says that the crux of verse 15 is the term ἀπεκδυσάμενος. Strictly, ἀπεκδύομαι ought to mean "take off," "strip off"; this is how it is understood by the oldest scholars. Some commentators have suggested τὴν σάρκα as the object, but the most natural interpretation is "having stripped off and put away the powers of evil." This is

---
153 Stott, 234.
154 Stott, 234.
155 Stott, 234.

— The Fullness of God in Christ: The Forgiver and Conqueror

accepted by Lightfoot. However, Leivestad further cites Lightfoot as admitting that the spiritual forces of evil, "which had clung like a Nessus robe about His humanity, were torn off and cast aside for ever."[156]

Leivestad adds that this interpretation of the term is strengthened by 2:11 and 3:9, but this has not been accepted by the larger number of modern commentators. They assign an active meaning to the verb. The meaning must then be that Christ, or God in Christ, has unclothed the powers, stripping them of the badge of their rank or of their arms.[157]

Leivestad points out that the determining factor for interpreting verse 15 is the understanding of the first participle in the verse, whether it refers to an action taken by God or whether it must be related to Christ. If Christ is the subject, then, "the rulers and authorities" is taken as the object of the following main verb, "he made an example of them." In this case, the implied object of "Christ stripped away (from himself)" is "his body," an interpretation favored by the Latin Fathers, Lightfoot, and adopted by J. A. T. Robinson.[158] Bratcher and Nida add that if ἀπεκδυσάμενος is taken as middle voice, it means "he stripped himself" or "caused himself to no longer be under the power of." If taken as an active, it means "he stripped the rulers and authorities" or he caused the rulers and authorities to no longer have power." The form is middle, but many understand it to have an active force.[159] Moule says that the middle voice is alleged

---

156 Leivestad, 103.
157 Leivestad, 103.
158 Bratcher and Nida, 61-62.
159 Bratcher and Nida, 62, 63.

Christ as Conqueror and Reconciler

to compel one to clarify what is meant by the Lord's stripping off something from Himself, that is, divesting Himself. Several interpretations have been offered, such as "having put off from himself His body." This explanation is supported by the Peshito Syriac version and by the following Church fathers: Ambrose, Hilary, and Augustine. The second interpretation: "Christ stripped away (from himself)" has reference to "his body." This version is offered by Lightfoot and supported by Chrysostom, Theodore of Mopsuestia, and other fathers. In the last explanation, the thought is that the powers of evil swarmed, so to speak, around Him who had taken our place under "the curse of the law," and that He in His triumph, stripped or cast them off.[160]

The opposition to the first interpretation is that it introduces a foreign and isolated idea that is in vague terms. The objection to the second explanation seems to be that it presents an image very peculiar in itself, and it is not clearly appropriate to the words that follow, that is, "to cast off enemies and then at once to exhibit them are not quite congruous ideas."[161]

Moule states that the lawful force of the middle voice would be as well represented by "stripping for Himself" as "stripping from Himself"; this makes the subject of the verb to be in some degree the object of the action: The Lord did "strip His foes for himself"; "He takes from him the armour (sic), and divided the spoils" (cf. Luke 11:22). The imagery is then congruent; the disarmed and the despoiled foes are then appropriate as captives, "shown" in triumph.[162]

---

160 H. C. G. Moule, "Studies in Colossians and Philemon," 107.
161 H. C. G. Moule, "Studies in Colossians and Philemon," 107.
162 H. C. G. Moule, "Studies in Colossians and Philemon," 107.

— The Fullness of God in Christ: The Forgiver and Conqueror

Stott, in recounting the phrase, says, "He made a public spectacle of them," exhibiting them as the "powerless powers" they now are and so "triumphing over them by the cross." This is most likely a reference to the procession of captives, which celebrated a victory. Alexander Maclaren offers a unified picture of Christ as "the victor stripping his foes of arms and ornaments and dress, then parading them as his captives, and then dragging them at the wheels of his triumphal car."[163] Bratcher and Nida add that this victory procession may be expressed as "as he rides along showing that he has been victorious" or "showing that he has conquered these powers" or ". . . these spirits." In view of the symbolic usage involved in this passage, it may be necessary to understand the phrase as a figure of speech, for example, "as though marching in triumph."[164]

Wilson shows that it was the situation in Colossae which leads Paul to show Christ's death on the cross as the crucial triumph over all the demonic powers of evil, for the false teaching which lifted up angels as the price of Christ clearly owed its insight to these defeated powers. Only Christ is Lord, and neither the good angels can lead the Colossians to God (1 Tim 2:5), nor the bad ones can separate them from Him (Rom 8:38-39). There is but one message of hope that relieves modern humankind of his or her frustration and despair. Wilson cites Bruce as contending that "Christ crucified and risen is Lord of all; all the forces of the universe are subject to Him, not only the benign ones but the hostile

---

163 Alexander Maclaren, "The Epistles of Paul to the Colossians and Philemon," *The Expositor's Bible* (Hodder & Stoughton, 1896), 222; quoted in Stott, 234, in agreement with Bratcher and Nida, 63 and H. C. G. Moule, "Studies in Colossians and Philemon," 107.
164 Bratcher and Nida, 63.

ones as well. They are all subject to Him as their Creator; the latter forces are subject to Him also as their Conqueror." Therefore, if one is united to Christ, he or she is delivered from his or her bondage, to enjoy the freedom of Him, to overcome all the power of evil because Christ's victory is humankind's (cf. Eph 6:10-18).[165] These "principalities and powers" have no more grip or power, for Christ overcame them all. He not only atones for and forgives sin, but he also conquers the hosts of evil.[166] Scholars are in agreement that "the rulers and authorities" are spiritual, supernatural, powers. Therefore, the TEV translates the phrase as the spiritual rulers and authorities.[167] Robertson, on the other hand, understands the powers to be angels such as the Gnostics worshipped, and the verb means to "despoil" rather than "having put off from himself."[168]

Jesus overcame the devil by totally resisting his temptations. Jesus was tempted to shun the cross, but He persevered in the path of obedience and became obedient to death—even death on the cross (Phil 2:8). His obedience was essential to His saving work. Paul in Romans says, "For just as through the disobedience of the one man the many were sinners, so also through the obedience of the one man the many will be made righteous" (Rom 5:19). Jesus was irritated by the insults and abuses to which He was subjected, but He totally refused to retaliate: "By His giving of Himself in love for others, he overcame evil with good" (Rom 12:21). When the combined forces of Rome and Jerusalem were lined up against Him,

---

165 Wilson, 56-57.
166 Pickell, 50-51.
167 Bratcher and Nida, 63.
168 Robertson, 495.

— The Fullness of God in Christ: The Forgiver and Conqueror

He could have met power with power. For Pilate had no final authority over Him; more than twelve legions of angels could have come to His assistance if He had summoned them, and He could have come down from the cross, as some in jest challenged Him to do. He decided against any use of worldly power. He was "crucified in weakness," though the weakness of God was stronger than any other force(s). Thus, He refused to disobey God, to hate His enemies, or to emulate the world's use of power. By His obedience, His love, and His meekness, He won a great moral victory over the powers of evil. He remained free, uncontaminated, uncompromised. The devil could gain no hold on Him and had to concede defeat. As F. F. Bruce puts it, "As he was suspended there, bound hand and foot to the wood in apparent weakness, they imagined they had him at their mercy, and thus flung themselves upon him with hostile intent.... But he grappled with them and mastered them. So the victory of Christ, predicted immediately after the Fall and begun during his public ministry, was decisively won at the cross."[169]

The death of Christ was not only a pardon; it also manifested might. It not only cancelled a debt, it was glorious triumph. By His cross the mighty Victor defeated Satan and all his hosts; Jesus despoiled them of their armor; He put them to open shame; He led them captive in triumph, "having despoiled the principalities and the powers, he made a show of them openly, triumphing over them in it." Why then fear the spiritual powers or the angelic beings before whom the false teachers bowed in worship? Why submit to Jewish rites and ceremonies? Christ alone is the Savior. He

---
169 Stott, 235.

Christ as Conqueror and Reconciler

is supreme. In Him is life. He meets every need.[170] H. C. G. Moule stated that "principalities and powers, literally, the governments and the authorities, the recognized enemies of Redemption and the Redeemer—these made their dire hostility supremely felt in that 'hour' which He Himself called 'the authority of the Darkness'" (Luke 22:53). The personal adversaries under their chief, who had crossed Jesus' path so often as the "demons" of possession, now directly attacked Himself, as they are still permitted in part to do (Eph 6:12). His followers meet them in Him, the Conqueror.[171] The Lord's atoning death, His obvious triumph over them, was seen in His resurrection "to be the mysterious Ransom of His Church from the curse and from sin and so His own glorification as its head." [172]

This whole passage, while saturated with primary and universal truth, has undoubtedly special reference to the "Colossian heresy" with its angelology and angelolatry. He who is king of all orders of good angels is here presented as Conqueror of their evil counterpart; He, from both points of view, meets the requirements.[173] In the cross of Christ, God showed His power openly without assistance from angels. He made a show of them by winning a complete victory over all the angelic agencies.[174]

It is especially in verse 15 that the idea of a mystical conflict and victory is clearly associated with the death of Jesus. The relation to verse 14 is obscure, as it is far from

---

170 Erdman, 70-71.
171 H. C. G. Moule, "Studies in Colossians and Philemon," 108.
172 H. C. G. Moule, "Studies in Colossians and Philemon," 108.
173 H. C. G. Moule, "Studies in Colossians and Philemon," 108.
174 Leivestad, 102-103.

— The Fullness of God in Christ: The Forgiver and Conqueror

evidence that the abrogation of humankind's debt and the Mosaic Law implies a triumph over "the principalities and powers."[175]

A question is whether ἐν αὐτῷ refers to the cross or to Christ. In favor of its referring to Christ is the fact that he is repeatedly referred to by pronouns six times in 2:10-13 and not less than four times in 1:19. In any case, it is most likely that Paul is thinking of the crucifixion. Leivestad cites Lohmeyer as contending that the illustration is not taken from the battlefield but from the royal court. It does not allude to the habit of stripping a beaten enemy of his arms but to the public humiliation of high officials. Leivestad cites Dibelius as even refusing to think of a battle-scene. Leivestad himself states that it is not of great importance whether one understands a shameful degradation of the powers, whereby their mantles and other symbols are taken from them or military conquest in which the victims are deprived of arms and weapons by the conqueror. The significant thing is that the crucifixion of Jesus, in one way or other, portrays a divine triumph over the cosmic powers.[176] The cosmic perspective of the atoning work of Christ is also brought out, by means of other metaphors, in Colossians 2:14-15. No other passage in Paul provides a stronger expression of the dramatic triumph of the crucified.[177]

Leivestad finds that the submission of the spirits are indicated also in Colossians 1:20. Percy maintains that the victory is gained on the cross and that verses 14 and 15 deal with the same event. The context is in favor of this view.[178]

---
175 Leivestad, 107.
176 Leivestad, 103-104.
177 Leivestad, 100.
178 E. Percy, *Die Probleme der Kolosser-und Epheserbriefe* (Lund, Sweden: C. W. K. Gleerup, 1946), 98; quoted in Leivestad, 104.

Christ as Conqueror and Reconciler

Leivestad does not understand the abrogation of the law as being equivalent to the triumph over the cosmic powers but says that it is surely very likely that the comparison between the law and the elemental spirits makes it easier to understand the correlation of the two.[179] It must be admitted that there are statements indirectly implying that the death of Jesus was caused by the law, in that Jesus submitted to the curse of the law. This seems to be a plausible inference from, among other passages, Colossians 2:14. But Colossians 2:14-15 is the only passage that actually indicates a direct connection between this aspect of the death of Jesus and the dramatic-mythical victory over the cosmic powers. The execution of Jesus can never be understood as a lawful act. He is not convicted according to the Mosaic Law. His condemnation cannot be acceptable through a legitimate reference to the law. Therefore, the law cannot be directly accountable for His death. When the cosmic powers cause the condemnation and death of Jesus, they act as usurpers. In so far as a juridical aspect may be combined with a mythical idea of conflict, it implies that the powers are themselves convicted and condemned.[180]

The following words of Stott are appropriate for summarizing and concluding this section:

> Two other important Pauline verses forge an indissoluble link between Christ's person and work, and so indicate that he was able to do what he did only because he was who he was. Both passages speak of

---
179 Leivestad, 104-105.
180 Leivestad, 105.

— The Fullness of God in Christ: The Forgiver and Conqueror

God's 'fullness' dwelling in him and working through him (Col 1:19-20; 2:9). This work is variously portrayed, but it is all attributed to the fullness of God residing in Christ—reconciling all things to himself, making peace by the blood of the cross, resurrecting us with Christ, forgiving all our sins, canceling the written code that was against us, taking it away, nailing it to the cross, and disarming the principalities and powers, triumphing over them either 'by it' (the cross) or 'in him' (Christ).[181]

---

181 Stott, 157, in agreement with Bruce, "Colossians Problems, Part 4: Christ as Conqueror and Reconciler," 293-294.

Part III

Chapter Four

Theological Implications for Deliverance

This chapter cites studies that deal with the theological implications for deliverance. Through Jesus' atonement, there is enough supportive evidence for each of the major atonement theories—Christus Victor, Legal Satisfaction, and Moral Influence—and deliverance healing.[182] In fact, deliverance is coherent with the essence of God's universal saving and cleansing work in creation which is made possible through Jesus Christ. The cleansing and restoring work is a direct result of Christ's death and resurrection.[183]

The most basic unifying theme throughout Jesus' ministry is that he was establishing the kingdom of God over against the kingdom of Satan. Jesus' healing and deliverance ministry comprised the initial victories over the enemy, while his death and resurrection imply Satan's final transfer of sovereignty. Yet, Jesus' victory over death was basically eschatological, that is, it pointed to a future time in which His achievement would be revealed in the fullest. Though Jesus' death in principle "drove out" the cosmic murderer (John 8:44),

---

182 Lawrence Burkholder, "The Theological Foundations of Deliverance Healing," *Conrad Grebel Review,* 19 (Winter 2001): 55.
183 Burkholder, 38-39.

Christ as Conqueror and Reconciler

this victory has not yet been fully made known in the world. Though Satan's stronghold has in principle been tottered and the strong man has been "tied up," his fortress has not yet fallen to the ground. Even though the authority to set people free from the bondages of the enemy has in principle been acknowledged and made accessible to all who accept and follow Christ, "the world is still held hostage by this, now mortally wounded and bound, strong man (1 John 5:19)."[184]

Christ was able to accomplish this because He dealt a death blow to Satan and recaptured his rightful rule over the whole creation. This is the essence of Jesus' ministry, death, and resurrection. Evil can be defeated in one's life only because the "evil one" who previously ruled the cosmos has himself in principle been conquered. Christians are liberated only because the whole universe has in principle been liberated from the one who had in the past imprisoned it. Also, Christians are reconciled to God only because the whole universe and the entire spiritual realm have in principle been reconciled to Him.[185]

In more graphic language, Boyd points out that through Jesus' death and resurrection, the previous "ruler of this world" has been "driven out" (John 12:31) and a new "leader," a legitimate ruler, has been installed in his place. Whereas the former ruler held humanity in misery, sin and bondage, this new Leader offers "repentance and forgiveness of sins" at no cost. Christ becomes the believers' "Savior" because He has become their "Leader" by expelling the old "ruler of the world" through his death on the cross.[186]

---

184 Boyd, 238-239.
185 Boyd, 267.
186 Boyd, 245.

Theological Implications for Deliverance

George E. Ladd also understands the death of Christ as being triumph over the cosmic powers. He continues by recognizing that Paul's worldview includes the concept of an invisible world of both good and evil spirits. People are in bondage not only to the law, sin, and death, but also to this evil, spiritual world. One of Christ's purposes for His mission was to destroy "every rule and every authority and power. For he must reign until he has put all his enemies under his feet" (1 Cor 15:24-25). In some mysterious way, the death of Christ comprised a primary defeat of these powers. This is clearly shown in Colossians: "When He had disarmed the rulers and authorities, He made a public example of them, having triumphing over them through Him" (Col 2:15). Consequently, the verse makes it plain that Christ was victorious over His spiritual enemies by His death, thus, accomplishing a decisive victory over the cosmic powers.[187]

David Garland understands that victory is accomplished when "all who have been buried in baptism with Christ have been set free from personal or impersonal powers that supposedly rule the universe. We have been set free from all those things that would have enslaved us, whether they be principles (worldly visions of what constitutes success) or principalities (other worldly or earthly forces)."[188]

Boyd, in discussing the benefits for Christians according to Colossians 2:15, states that it is clearly speaking about

---

187 George E. Ladd, *A Theology of the New Testament* (Grand Rapids, MI: William B. Eerdmans Publishing Company, 1993), 476-477.
188 David E. Garland, "Colossians/Philemon," *The NIV Application Commentary*, vol. 36 (Grand Rapids, MI: Bondservant Publishing House, 1998), 171, in agreement with Ralph Martin, *Colossians: The Church's Lord and the Christian's Liberty* (Grand Rapids, MI: Zondervan Publishing House, 1972), 87.

Christ as Conqueror and Reconciler

the importance of the cross for believers by combining its anthropocentric and cosmic dimensions. The cross triumphed over God's enemies. The war that had been waged for eons was now in principle completed. This means that there is full and unrestricted freedom. Believers are no longer slaves to demonic censure, for everything for which Satan and his minions could ever condemn persons was destroyed in the same act that destroyed them.[189]

Indeed, Paul could go so far in expressing believers' freedom from demonic powers as to say that Christians "have died with Christ to the elemental principles of the world" (2:20). Even more, Paul insists that in Him [Christ] Christians "have been made complete, and He is the head of all rule and authority" (Col 2:10). Not only are Christians dead to demonic powers; they have within them, according to Paul, the very same power over them that Christ Himself has.[190]

The most fundamental reality from which believers are set free is the devil. Persons were enslaved to sin and condemnation primarily because they were slaves to Satan. In redeeming persons out of this bondage, in rescuing them out of this kingdom (Col 1:13; Gal 1:4), Christ in principle bought persons out of every other form of bondage as well. The price of this redemption, Peter says, was not ". . . with perishable things like silver or gold . . . , but with [the] precious blood . . . of Christ" (1 Pet 1:18, 19).[191]

Bruce states that if one suddenly becomes aware that he or she is being moved by ideas to adopt standards which are

---

189 Boyd, 261.
190 Boyd, 261-262.
191 Boyd, 266.

less than Christian, he or she should recognize these influences to be inimical forces from which he or she must seek deliverance, which is available because it has already been secured.[192]

In continuing Bruce says that these may be impersonal forces or demons under the power of Satan, the personal "prince of the power of the air" (Eph 2:2). Individuals whose faith is in Christ, the conqueror, will not underrate the strength and malignity of such forces; but they will recognize them to be defeated forces. Christ who was crucified and raised from the dead is Lord of all. Though believers do not as yet see all things put under Him, to be united to Him by faith is to share His victory here and now and to benefit from the deliverance from the forces he has overcome.[193]

For Christians as for Christ, life means conflict. For Christians as for Christ, it also means victory—they are to be victorious like Christ was victorious. John writes to the "young men" of the churches he supervised because they had "overcome the evil one." Jesus purposefully shows a parallel between Himself and humankind by promising to him or her who overcomes the right to share His throne, just as He had overcome and shared His Father's throne.[194]

Yet, the parallel is only partial. It would be entirely impossible for persons by themselves to fight and conquer the devil. They lack both the skill and the strength to do so. It is also unnecessary to make the attempt, because Christ has already

---

[192] Bruce, "Colossians Problems, Part 4: Christ as Conqueror and Reconciler," 299.
[193] Bruce, "Colossians Problems, Part 4: Christ as Conqueror and Reconciler," 300.
[194] Stott, 239.

Christ as Conqueror and Reconciler

done it. The victory of Christians, therefore, is found in entering into the victory of Christ and profiting from its benefits. Christian can thank God that He "gives us the victory through our Lord Jesus Christ" (1 Cor 15:57). They know that Jesus, having been raised from the dead, is now seated at the right hand of the Father in the heavenly places. But God has "made us alive together with Christ . . . , and raised us up with Him, and seated us with Him in the heavenly places" (Eph 1: 20-23). In other words, by God's gracious power, persons who have shared in Christ's resurrection share also in His throne. If God has placed all things under Christ's feet, they must be under Christians' as well, if they are in Him (Eph 2:4-6). To borrow Jesus' own figure of speech, now that the strong man has been disarmed and bound, the time is ready for believers to invade his palace and take his goods (Mk 3:27).[195]

It is not quite that easy, however. For though the devil has been defeated, he has not yet conceded defeat. Although he has been toppled, he has not yet been destroyed. In fact, he continues to wield great power. This is the reason that believers feel tension in both their theology and their experience. Persons who have been born of God are alive, kept safe, "and the evil one does not touch them, seated and reigning with Christ, as has just been seen, with even the principalities and powers of evil placed by God under His feet, and, therefore, Christians as well."[196]

For the Colossians, as for many subsequently, these oppressing forces still seems to be loosed within the world and exercising power over people. How can one say, then,

---

[195] Stott, 239.
[196] Stott, 239-240.

Theological Implications for Deliverance

that they have been defeated? The cross guarantees their defeat and takes God's program even further in the consummation of the ages when they will be totally destroyed and every eye shall see it when Christ returns in glory. But we have not yet reached its completion.[197]

Stott's six stages of God's program helps at this point: "Stage one is the conquest predicted, from Genesis 3:15 onwards. Stage two is the conquest begun, in the ministry of Jesus. Stage three is the conquest achieved, in the death of Jesus. Stage four is the conquest confirmed, in the resurrection of Jesus. Stage five is the conquest extended, through the Church of Jesus. Stage six is the conquest consummated, by the return of Jesus."[198] Believers are now in stage five, where the conquest is extended through the Church of Jesus.

Tidball declares that Christians have a victory to celebrate and proclaim with assurance, even now that they have become apprehensive of triumphalism. The hesitancy and mediocrity of much Christian living today may, indeed, be specifically due to Christian's lack of teaching and believing that Christ really has already won the victory over their enemies through his cross. It is not a victory in which he needs human assistance, as they engage in fighting the enemy, but one He could and did win on His own, and through which he offers assistance to believers. It is a victory not just to celebrate but to experience, as, taking refuge in the cross of Christ, Christians can now resist their enemies and walk in freedom.[199]

---

197 Stott, 239-240.
198 Stott, 231-239.
199 Tidball, 260-261.

Stott states that many Christians choose one or the other of these positions, or vacillate unsteadily between them. Some are triumphalists, who see only the decisive victory of Jesus Christ and overlook the apostolic warnings against the powers of darkness. Others are defeatists, who see only the fearsome malice of the devil and overlook the victory over him which Christ has already won. The tension is part of the Christian dilemma between the "already" and the "not yet." Already the kingdom of God has been inaugurated and is advancing; not yet has it been consummated. Already the new age (the age to come) has come, so that one has "tasted… the powers of the coming age"; not yet has the old age completely passed away. Already Christians are sons and daughters, and no longer slaves; not yet have they entered "the glorious freedom of the children of God." An overemphasis on the "already" leads to triumphalism, the claim to perfection—either moral perfection or complete physical health—which belongs only to the consummated kingdom, the "not yet." Too much emphasis on the "not yet" leads to defeatism, a submission in continuing evil which is incompatible with the "already" of Christ's victory.[200] Satan has been bound but not demolished. He is not powerless but his power has been weakened.[201] Steven Voorwinde further quotes G. E. Ladd as stating that "the decisive battle in the war has been won, but the final victory is yet to be gained. The whole mission of Jesus meant an initial defeat of satanic power that makes the final outcome and triumph of God's kingdom certain. Every occasion in which Jesus drives out an evil spirit is a foretaste of the eschaton."[202]

---

200 Stott, 240.
201 Steven Voorwinde, "Demons and the Occult in the New Testament," *Vox Reformata* 59 (1994): 36.
202 G. E. Ladd, *The Theology of the New Testament* (Grand Rapids: Eerdmans, 1974), 66; quoted in Voorwinde, 30.

Theological Implications for Deliverance

It is not until Stott's sixth stage of God's program, called the *conquest consummated,* will Christ's death on the cross have its full effect over Satan and his evil dominion, authority, and power. This is now the period of time between the two advents when the Church is to be involved in its mission. Christ is already reigning, but in the consummation of the ages His enemies will become His footstool.[203] At the consummation, ". . . He hands over the kingdom to the God and Father, when He has abolished all rule and all authority and power" (1 Cor 15:24). The cosmic redemption will be complete, and, with the vanishing of the "powers," the semidemonic state will also disappear as it is known.[204] Steven Voorwinde points out that the triumph of God's kingdom over the domination of Satan is nowhere stated as clearly as it is in Revelation 11:15 and 12:10. There the contrasts are sharply drawn and the victory is final and total. Revelation tells of the completion of Jesus' kingdom victory where "the D-Day of the cross and resurrection have led to the V-Day of the consummation."[205] Satan and his minions are finally destroyed. Therefore, "The kingdom of God and the authority of His Christ have come" (12:10) and the "kingdom of the world has become the kingdom of our Lord, and of His Christ; and He will reign forever and ever (11:15)."[206]

---

203 Stott, 236
204 G. H. C. MacGregor, "Principles and Powers: The Cosmic Background of Paul's Thought," *New Testament Studies* 1 (1954-55): 25.
205 Voorwinde, 36.
206 Voorwinde, 38.

Chapter Five

The Church's Role in Deliverance

This chapter discusses the Church's role in deliverance ministry today and then summarizes and concludes the study. It is possible that the vision of Yahweh as a Divine Warrior was an important influence on the Christology of the early Church, and the theme may offer a hint to the messianic self-understanding of Jesus.[207] Because of Christ's victory over and reconciliation of evil powers, or forces, through His death on the cross, deliverance is possible and available because it has already been secured.[208] In fact, it is a ministry which Jesus mandates His disciples (Church) to continue today[209]—". . . God was in Christ reconciling the world to Himself, not counting their trespasses against them, and he has committed to us the word of reconciliation. Therefore, we are ambassadors for Christ, as though God were making an appeal through us" (2 Cor 5:19-20a).

---

207 Bruce A. Stevens, "Jesus as the Divine Warrior," *Expository Times* 94 (1983): 326.
208 Bruce, "Colossian Problem, Part 4: Christ as Conqueror and Reconciler," 299.
209 Burkholder, 39.

Christ as Conqueror and Reconciler

Even though the Epistles do not make mention of exorcisms, they do bring out the fuller dimensions of the spiritual warfare in which the whole Church is involved. Because of Christ's decisive victory over His enemies, the Church is equipped with His armor and enters the battle with assurance.[210]

The consummation of Christ's victory is bound up with the reconciling work which He has already accomplished on the Cross. His victory is seen in the lives of believers, who are reconciled to God through Him and are now on the Lord's side in the conflict of the ages. Because the decisive battle has been fought and won, they know that the final matter is not in question. At present, their lives are hid with Christ in God, and when Christ, who is their life, is manifested, they will be manifested with Him in glory (Col 3:4).[211]

That is not the end of the story. The letter to the Colossians has as its companion and sequel the letter to the Ephesians. If Christ fills the cosmic role ascribed to Him in Colossians, what part is played in this cosmic clash by those who are united in Him, "the Church which is his body" (Eph 1:22-23)? To this question Ephesians provides the answer, for Ephesians is "Paul's message for today," aiming to "present Pauline teaching in it universal and eternal aspect."[212] In Ephesians 3:10, the Church is assigned an important role at the heart of the revelation of the mystery of God's intention for the universe. In fact, it is the avenue by which God makes

---

210 Voorwinde, 37.
211 Bruce, "Colossians Problems, Part 4: Christ as Conqueror and Reconciler," 300.
212 C. Leslie Mitton, *Ephesians* (London: Oliphants, 1976), 11, 29; quoted in Mark Kiley, *Colossians as Pseudepigraphy: The Biblical Seminar* (Sheffield, England: JSOT Press, 1986), 103.

The Church's Role in Deliverance

known His wisdom to the principalities and authorities.[213] As the Church is reminded of its salvation, it is told in Ephesians 2:10 that it is God's work, and it has been created for good works through its activity in Christ.[214] The Church, in Ephesians, is God's masterpiece of reconciliation; it is comprised of those who also have been individually reconciled to God through Christ and who have been reconciled through the Cross of Christ to each other "in one body" (Eph 2:14-16). Through this masterpiece of reconciliation, "the rulers and the authorities in the heavenly places" are intended to learn "the manifold wisdom of God" (Eph 3:10) by which He conceived "the plan of the mystery hidden for ages" (Eph 3:9). This plan, to be understood in the fullness of time, considers the uniting in Christ of "all things . . . things in heaven and things on earth" (Eph 1:10). The Church, in spite of all its restrictions which are at present so apparent, is God's advance replica of the wider and more comprehensive fellowship of reconciliation which is yet to be realized. More than that, the Church, as the Body of Christ, is God's agency for bringing this comprehensive fellowship into being. God's plan to sum all things up in Christ involves the ministry and witness of those that are already in Him.[215]

Bruce further says that when Paul told the Corinthians that, because of their spiritual immaturity, he had to feed them with milk and not with solid food, he declared that among the mature he had a wisdom to impart—"the wisdom of God in a mystery, the hidden wisdom which God

---

213 Andrew T. Lincoln and A. J. M. Wedderburn, *The Theology of the Later Pauline Letters* (Cambridge: The Cambridge University Press, 1993), 93.
214 Lincoln and Wedderburn, 93.
215 Bruce, "Colossians Problems, Part 4: Christ as Conqueror and Reconciler," 300-301.

decreed before the ages for our glory" (1 Cor 2:7). Since an explanation of this wisdom is not provided in the Corinthian letter, it is given in Colossians and Ephesians.[216]

Boyd points out that this wisdom that Christians are to clearly manifest "includes the deliverance of humans from Satan's kingdom (Col 1:13)"; therefore, they are to be "vitally interested in saving individual souls." In dissimilarity to much of "modern conservative Christian thinking," the salvation of persons does not exhaust the substance of what the Church is to be about as it "proclaim God's manifold wisdom." Conversely, as has been seen, the wisdom made known in Christ Jesus, the very wisdom Christians are to proclaim, "was cosmic before it was anthropological."[217] Boyd also states that if the Church "misses the cosmic aspect of evil itself; it misses the cosmic dimension of the Church's calling to revolt against all forms of evil in order to demonstrably proclaim Jesus' victory over them."[218]

So Paul could encourage the Christians at Colosse to give "thanks to the Father, who has qualified us to share in the inheritance of the saints in light" (Col 1:12). He then tells them the basis of this qualification: "... He has rescued us from the domain of darkness and transferred us into the kingdom of His beloved Son, in whom we have redemption, the forgiveness of sins" (Col 1:13-14).[219]

As other New Testament authors realized, "this means there is still work to be done, and the Church is the means

---

216 Bruce, "Colossians Problems, Part 4: Christ as Conqueror and Reconciler," 301.
217 Boyd, 253-254.
218 Boyd, 267.
219 Boyd, 239.

The Church's Role in Deliverance

by which it is to be done." In the meantime "between the 'already' of Christ's work and the 'not yet' of the eschaton, the Church is to be about what Jesus was about. It is, in a real sense, His 'body' here on earth. As such, the Church is to be an extension of the ministry He Himself carried out in His Incarnate body while here on earth (2 Cor 5:18-19)."[220]

The Church "is to manifest the truth that God's Kingdom has come and that Satan's kingdom is defeated. Thus, in its own way, under the victorious authority of Christ," the Church is to take on and overthrow evil powers, just as Jesus Himself did. In fact, when the Church "does this through the Spirit, it is Jesus Himself who is doing it." This is the reason, in spite of His disciples' enthusiastic assurance in the completed work of the cross, one does "not find the warfare worldview of Jesus lessened one iota among them."[221]

Dana Keener also stresses that one way deliverance can be accomplished more effectively is through the power and guidance of the Holy Spirit. This procedure emphasizes the importance of one's daily relationship with God rather than concern for technique. This method also allows for diversity in how deliverance is carried out. When the Holy Spirit leads the way, this allows for freedom and creativity in the act of deliverance.[222]

In fact, the nature and dimension of the spiritual conflict is portrayed in its greatest complexity in Ephesians 6:10-18. There the issue is both wider and more subtle than as merely a matter of casting out demons. Christians are advised that

---
220 Boyd, 239.
221 Boyd, 239.
222 Dana Keener, "Response to Lawrence Burkholder," *Conrad Grebel Review* 19 (Winter 2001): 76.

a war is in session, which cannot be fought by human means or with earthly resources. In this spiritual warfare, every Christian is admonished to put on "the full armor of God" (Eph 6:11, 13).[223] Voorwinde further states that the genitive is subjective, that is, it is the outfit which God supplies. Paul's allusions to the Old Testament indicate that this is the armor that God Himself wears. In Isaiah 59:17, it is Yahweh who "put on righteousness like a breastplate, And a helmet of salvation on His head" (cf. Eph 6:15, 17). Likewise, the Messiah is armed with truth, righteousness, and the Gospel of peace (Isa 11:5; 52:7; cf. Eph 6:14, 15). Isaiah's simile finds its fulfillment in the redemptive work of Christ and continues in the spiritual warfare of the messianic community. The "decisive battle has been won, but the war goes on, and the foot-soldiers are to wear the armour (*sic*) of the King!"[224]

In summarizing this chapter, Tidball's words concerning Stott's level five are worth quoting:

> When the gospel must be announced but during which the powers will not concede their defeat. They pretend that their fictitious strength is unaffected and, even in their death throes, they continue to hold unbelievers captive and to hassle believers. They have no right to do so, but they are so practised (sic) in the art of deception that they do not even realize that they have been vanquished. It is for this very reason that we must announce the gospel. We must let people know that Christ has opened the prison doors and taken our

---

223 Voorwinde, 34.
224 Voorwinde, 34.

would-be jailers captive. We must announce the triumph of Christ to unbelievers and believers alike, so that the former may come into an initial experience of the liberating power of the cross and the latter may continue to experience the fullness of the liberation Christ brings. Here, Paul has the latter particularly in view. Believers lacked the confidence to shake off these hostile powers. Did they not realize that "The unseen powers and invisible forces that had dominated and determined so much of life need no longer be feared. A greater power and force was at work which could rule and determine their lives more efficiently—in a word, "Christ." Triumph indeed![225]

---

225 Tidball, 260-261.

Summary and Conclusion of the Study

This study set out to show the close relationship between the portrayal of Christ as Reconciler in Colossians 1:19-20 and the depiction of Him as Conqueror in Colossians 2:13-15. It was found that Christ fulfilled both of these roles because the fullness of God abided in Him. Through Christ's death on the cross, He was both able to reconcile all things—cosmically and individually—to Himself and be victorious—cosmically and individually—over all His enemies. Because of His reconciling and victorious work cosmically, one can individually experience deliverance from evil beings or forces now and is encouraged through the Church to continue this ministry, waiting for the fuller manifestation of it at the consummation of the ages.

Bibliography

Books

Abbot, T. K. *A Critical and Exegetical Commentary on the Epistles to the Ephesians and the Colossians.* The International Critical Commentary. Vol. 36. New York: Charles Scribner's Sons, 1897.

Aland, Barbara, Kurt Alan, Johannes Karavidopoulos, Carlo M. Martini, and Bruce M. Metzger, eds. *The Greek New Testament.* Stuttgart, Germany: United Bible Societies, 2001.

Aulờn, Gustaf. *Christus Victor: A Historical Study of the Three Main Types of the Idea of Atonement.* London: Society for Promoting Christian Knowledge, 1931. Reprint, New York: MacMillan, 1967.

Beare, Francis W., and G. Preston MacLeod. "The Epistle to the Colossians." *The Interpreter's Bible.* Vol. 11. Edited by George A. Buttrick. Reprint, Nashville, TN: Abingdon Press, 1955, 1983.

Boyd, Gregory A. *God at War: The Bible & Spiritual Conflict.* Downers Groves, IL: InterVarsity Press, 1997.

Bratcher, Robert G., and Eugene A. Nida. *A Handbook on Paul's Letters to the Colossians and to Philemon.* New York: United Bible Societies, 1977.

Bruce, Frederick F. "The Epistles to Colossians, to Philemon, and to the Ephesians." *The New International Commentary on the New Testament.* Vol. 10B. Grand Rapids, MI: William B. Eerdmans Publishing Company, 1984. 3187.

_____. *Paul: Apostle of the Heart Set Free.* Grand Rapids, MI: William B. Eerdmans Publishing Company, 1977.

Danker, Frederick William, ed. *A Greek-English Lexicon of the New Testament and Other Early Christian Literature.* Chicago, IL: The University of Chicago Press, 2000.

Elwell, Walter A., ed. *Evangelical Dictionary of Theology.* 2d ed. Grand Rapids, MI: Baker House Company, 2001.

Erdman, Charles R. *The Epistles of Paul to the Colossians and to Philemon: An Exposition*. Philadelphia: The Westminster Press, 1933.

Fahlbusch, Erwin, and Geoffrey William Bromiley, eds. *The Encyclopedia of Christianity*. Vol 1. Grand Rapids, MI: William B. Eerdmans Publishing Co., 1999.

Garland, David E. "Colossians/Philemon." *The NIV Application Commentary*. Vol. 36. Grand Rapids, MI: Zondervan Publishing House, 1998. 17-291.

Jeremias, Joachim. *Central Message of the New Testament*. London: SCM Press (1966), 37. Quoted in John R. Stott, *The Cross of Christ*. Downers Grove, IL: InterVarsity Press (1986), 233-234.

Kiley, Mark. *Colossians as Pseudepigraphy: The Biblical Seminar*. Sheffield, England: JSOT Press, 1986.

Ladd, G. E. *The Theology of the New Testament*. Grand Rapids: MI: Eerdmans, 1974. 66. Quoted in Steven Vooruinde, "Demons and the Occult in the New Testament." *Voh Reformata* 59 (1994): 30.

_____. *A Theology of the New Testament*. Rev. ed. Edited by Donald A. Hagner. Grand Rapids, MI: William B. Eerdmans, 1993.

Leivestad, Ragnar. *Christ the Conqueror: Ideas of Conflict and Victory in the New Testament*. New York: The Macmillan Company, 1954.

Lightfoot, J. B. *Saint Paul's Epistles to the Colossians and to Philemon*. Grand Rapids, MI: Zondervan Publishing House, 1961.

Lincoln, Andrew T., and A. J. M. Wedderburn. *The Theology of the Later Pauline Letters*. Cambridge: The Cambridge University Press, 1993.

Maclaren, Alexander. "The Epistles of Paul to the Colossians and Philemon." *The Expositor's Bible*. Hedder & Stoughton, 1896, 222. Quoted in John Stott, *The Cross of Christ*, 234, Downers Grove, IL: InterVarsity Press, 1986.

Martin, Ralph P. "Colossians and Philemon." *New Century Bible*. Edited by Ronald E. Clements and Matthew Black. Greenwood, SC: The Attic Press, Inc., 1974.

Bibliography

_____. *Colossians: The Church's Lord and the Christian's Liberty.* Grand Rapids, MI: Zondervan Publishing House, 1972.

Martin, Ralph P. "Reconciliation and Forgiveness in Colossians." *Reconciliation and Hope: New Testament Essays on Atonement and Eschatology.* Edited by Robert Banks, 104-124. Grand Rapids, MI: William B. Eerdmans Publishing Company, 1974.

Metzger, Bruce M. *The Text of the New Testament.* New York: Oxford University Press, 1968.

_____. *A Textual Commentary on the Greek New Testament.* New York: United Bible Societies, 1971.

Mitton, C. Leslie. *Ephesians.* London: Oliphants, 1976, 11, 29. Quoted in Mark Kiley, *Colossians as Pseudepigraphy: The Biblical Seminar,* 103. Sheffield, England: JSOT Press, 1986.

Moule, C. F. D. *The Epistles of Paul the Apostle to the Colossians and to Philemon.* Cambridge Greek Testament Commentary. Edited by C. F. D. Moule. Cambridge: The Cambridge University Press, 1958.

Moule, H. C. G. *Colossians and Philemon Studies.* Minneapolis, MN: Klock & Klock Christian Publishers, Inc., 1981, 9. Quoted in Curtis Vaughn, *Colossians and Philemon.* Bible Study Commentary, 11. Grand Rapids, MI: Zondervan Publishing House, 1980.

_____. *Studies in Colossians & Philemon.* Grand Rapids, MI: Kregel Publications, 1977.

O'Brien, Peter T. "Colossians, Philemon." *Word Biblical Commentary.* Vol. 44. Waco, TX: Word Books, Publisher, 1982, xxv-261.

Percy, E. *Die Probleme der Kolosser und Epheserbriefe.* Lund, Sweden: C. W. K. Gleerup, 1946, 98. Quoted in Ragnar Leivestad, *Christ the Conqueror: Ideas of Conflict and Victory in the New Testament,* 104. New York: The Macmillan Company, 1954.

Pickell, Charles N. *The Epistle to the Colossians: A Study Manual.* Grand Rapids, MI: Baker Book House, 1965.

Richardson, Alan, ed. *A Dictionary of Christian Theology.* Philadelphia: The Westminster Press, 1969.

Richardson, Alan, and John Bowen, eds. *The Westminster Dictionary of Christian Theology*. Philadelphia: The Westminster Press, 1983.

Rienecker, Fritz. "Colossians." *A Linguistic Key to Greek New Testament*. Vol. 2. Edited by Cleon L.Rogers, Jr. Grand Rapids, MI: Zondervan Publishing House, 1980. 218-239.

Robertson, A. T. *Word Pictures in the New Testament*. Vol. 4. Nashville, TN: Broadman Press, 1930.

Rogers, Jr., Cleon L., and Cleon L. Rogers, III. *The New Linguistic and Exegetical Key to the Greek New Testament*. Grand Rapids, MI: Zondervan Publishing House, 1998.

Rogers, Patrick V. "Colossians." *New Testament Message: A Biblical-Theological Commentary*. Vol. 15. Edited by Winfrid Harrington and Donald Senior. Wilmington, DE: Michael Glazier, Inc., 1980. ix-98.

Stagg, Frank. *The Holy Spirit Today*. Nashville, TN: Broadman Press, 1973.

_____. *New Testament Theology*. Nashville, TN: Broadman Press, 1962.

Stott, John R. *The Cross of Christ*. Downers Grove, IL: InterVarsity Press, 1986.

Taylor, Vincent. *Forgiveness and Reconciliation: A Study in New Testament Theology*. London: Macmillan and Company, Limited, 1946.

Tidball, Derek. *The Message of the Cross*. Downers Grove, IL: InterVarsity Press, 2001.

Twerski, Abraham J. *Addictive Thinking: Understanding Self-Deception*. 2d ed. Center City, MN: Hazelden Foundation, 1997.

Vaughn, Curtis. "Colossians." *The Expositor's Bible Commentary*. Vol. 11. Edited by Frank E. Gaebelein. Grand Rapids, MI: Zondervan Publishing House, 1978. 163-226.

_____. *Colossians and Philemon*. Bible Study Commentary. Grand Rapids, MI: Zondervan Publishing House, 1980.

Webber, Robert E. *The Church in the World: Opposition, Tension or Transformation?* Grand Rapids, MI: Academie/Zondervan, 1986.

White, R. E. O. "Colossians." *The Broadman Bible Commentary.* Vol. 11. Edited by Clifton J. Allen. Nashville, TN: Broadman Press, 1971. 217-256.

Wilson, Geoffrey B. *Colossians and Philemon.* Carlisle, PA: The Banner of Truth Trust, 1980.

Yates, Roy. *The Epistle to the Colossians.* Edited by Ivor H. Jones. London: Epworth Press, 1993.

Yeager, Randolph O. *The Renaissance New Testament.* Vol. 15. Gretna, LA: Pelican Publishing Co., 1998.

Periodicals

Bruce, Frederick F. "Colossian Problems, Part 1: Jews and Christians in the Lycus Valley." *Bibliotheca Sacra* 141 (1984): 3-15. ATLA Religious Database, EBSCOhost (21 November 2005).

_____. "Colossians Problems, Part 2: The 'Christ Hymn' of Colossians 1:15-20." *Bibliotheca Sacra* 141 (1984): 99-111. ATLA Religious Database, EBSCOhost (21 November 2005).

_____. "Colossians Problems, Part 3: The Colossians Heresy." *Bibliotheca Sacra* 141 (1984): 195-208. ATLA Religious Database, EBSCOhost (21 November 2005).

_____. "Colossian Problems, Part 4: Christ as Conqueror and Reconciler." *Bibliotheca Sacra* 141 (1984): 291-302. ATLA Religious Database, EBSCOhost (13 October 2005).

Burkholder, Lawrence. "The Theological Foundations of Deliverance Healing." *Conrad Grebel Review* 19 (Winter 2001): 38-68.

Keener, Dana. "Response to Lawrence Burkholder." *Contrad Grebel Review* 19 (Winter 2001): 74-78.

MacGregor, G. H. C. "Principalities and Powers: The Cosmic Background of Paul's Thought." *New Testament Studies* 1 (1954-55): 17-28.

Moule, C. F. D. "Obligation in the Ethic of Paul." *Christian History and Interpretation.* Edited by W. R. Farmer, C. F. D. Moule, and R. R. Niebuhr. New York: Cambridge University Press, 1967, 392. Quoted in F. F. Bruce, "Colossians Problems. Part 4: Christ as Conqueror and Reconciler." *Bibliotheca Sacra* 141 (1984): 295. ATLA Religious Database, EBSCOhost (13 October 2005).

Nash, J. Madeleine. "The Chemistry of Addiction." *Time* 5 (May 1997): 68-72, 74, 76.

Stevens, Bruce A. "Jesus as the Divine Warrior." *The Expository Times* 94 (1983): 326-329.

Voorwinde, Steven. "Demons and the Occult in the New Testament." *Vox Reformata* 59 (1994): 17-38.

Other Sources

Mansfield, M. Robert. "Class Study Guide: New Testament Hermeneutics and Exegesis." Class notes from GBIB 581 New Testament Hermeneutics and Exegesis, Oral Roberts University, Fall 2004.

_____. "Textual Criticism: Criteria for Evaluating Variants." Class notes from GBIB 581 New Testament Hermeneutics and Exegesis. Oral Roberts University, Fall 2004.

Schweitzer, Eduard. "Christ in the Letter to the Colossians." *Review and Expositor* 70 (1973): 456-457. Quoted in James Albert Weaver, "Colossians 1:15-20 and Its Function in the Letter." Ph.D. diss., The Southern Baptist Theological Seminary, School of Theology, 1982. University Microfilms International, 5420 (1982).

Weaver, James Albert. "Colossians 1:15-20 and Its Function in the Letter." Ph.D. diss., The Southern Baptist Theological Seminary, School of Theology, 1982. University Microfilms International, 5420 (1982).

Greek Index

αἵματος 27
αἴρω 41
ἀκροβυτίᾳ 37
ἀπεκδύομαι 46
ἀπεκδυσάμενος 46, 47
ἀποκαταλλάξαι 27
ἀποκαταλλάσσω 28
ἀρχας 46
αὐτὸ 39
αὐτόν 27
αὐτοῦ 27
αὐτοὺς 46
αὐτῷ 23, 37, 38, 46, 53

γῆς 27
γράφω 40

δι' 27
διά 13, 27
δόγμασιν 39, 42

ἐδειγμάτισεν 46
εἰρηνοποιήσας 27
εἰς 27
εἴτε 27
ἐκ 39
ἐν 13, 23, 27, 37, 46, 53
ἐξαλείψας 39
ἐξουσίας 46
ἐπὶ 27
εὐδόκησεν 23, 25

ζάω 38

ζώ 38

ἦρκεν 38, 39
ἡμᾶς 37
ἡμῖν 37, 38, 39
ἦν 13, 39
ἡμῶν 39

θεός 25, 38
θριαμβεύσας 46

καὶ 27, 37, 39, 46
καθ' 39
καταλλαγὴ 13
καταλλαγή 16
καταλλάσσω 28
καταλλάσσων 13
καταργέω 44
καρίζομαι 38
κάρις 38
κατοικῆσαι 23, 25
κόσμος 13, 14
κόσμου 13

μέσου 39

νεκροὺς 37

ὁ 25
ὃ 39
ὄντας 37
ὅτι 23
οὐρανοῖς 27

85

Christ as Conqueror and Reconciler

πᾶν 23, 25
πάντα 27, 37
παραπτώμασιν 37
παραπτώματα 37
παρρησίᾳ 46
πλήρωμα 23, 25
ποιέω 38
προσηλώσας 39

σάρκα 46
σαρκὸς 37
σταυροῦ 27
σταυρῷ 39
συζωοποιέω 38
σύν 37, 38
συνεζωοποίησεν 37

τὰ 27, 37
τὰς 46

τῇ 37
τὴν 46
τῆς 27, 37
τὸ 23, 25, 39
τοῖς 27, 37, 39, 42
τοῦ 27, 39
τῷ 39

ὑμᾶς 37
ὑμῖν 37
ὑμῶν 37
ὑπεναντίον 39

χάρις 38
χαρίζομαι 38
χαρισάμενος 37
χείρ 40
χειρόγραφον 39, 40, 41, 43, 46

Scripture Index

Genesis
3:15....................65

Psalm
51:9.....................40
109:14..................40

Isaiah
11:5.....................74
43:25...................40
52:7.....................74
59:17...................74

Mark
3:27.....................64

Luke
4:18.....................16
11:22...................48
22:53...................52

John
1:18.....................22
1:29.....................40
3:16-17................13
8:44.....................59
12:31...................60
12:47...................13

Acts
16:31...................16
19:10....................2

28:30....................2

Romans
2:14-15................41
3:31...............44, 45
4-7.......................9
5:1......................13
5:9-11...................2
5:10....................12
5:11...............12, 16
5:19....................50
7:12....................43
8:19-21................30
8:21....................13
8:38-39................49
11:15...........2, 13, 14
12:21...................50

1 Corinthians
2:7.....................72
15.......................9
15:20..................22
15:24..................67
15:24-25..............61
15:57..................64

2 Corinthians
3:7-16.................44
5:16-21.................2
5:18............9, 12, 14
5:18-19................73
5:19........9, 12, 13, 14, 29
5:19-20a...............69

87

5:20.................12
5:21.................43

Galatians
1:4..................62
3:10-13..............9
3:13.................43
3:19-4:4.............44

Ephesians
1:7-10...............16
1:10............27, 31, 33, 71
1:20-23..............64
1:22.................33
1:22-23..............70
1:23.................24
2:2...............38, 63
2:3..................38
2:4f.................38
2:4-6................64
2:5..................38
2:8..................16
2:10.................71
2:11-12..............39
2:11-22..............2
2:13.................38
2:14..............38, 42
2:14-16..............71
2:15.................44
2:15-16..............13
2:16.................29
3:9..................71
3:10..............70, 71
3:19.................24

4:2..................38
4:13.................24
4:31.................38
4:32.................38
6:10-18...........50, 73
6:11.................74
6:12.................52
6:13.................74
6:14.................74
6:15.................74
6:17.................74
6:21..................3

Philippians
2:8..................50
2:9-11...............33

Colossians
1....................27
1:7...................2
1:8...................2
1:9..................26
1:9-15...............36
1:10-13..............38
1:12...............3, 72
1:13..............62, 72
1:13-14..............72
1:15-20......14, 16, 21, 22, 29, 31, 32, 33, 83, 84
1:16..........5, 6, 14, 22, 27
1:18a................36
1:19..14, 23, 24, 25, 26, 27, 53
1:19-20.......... ix, 1, 21, 26, 28, 35, 55, 77

1:20............14, 26, 27, 28,
       29, 32, 35, 42, 53
1:21..........................3, 31
1:21-23 28
1:22..................................29
1:24....................................2
1:27....................................3
2:1......................................2
2:6-7 6
2:8......................................5
2:8-15 ....14, 36
2:9............14, 24, 25, 26, 55
2:10............5, 6, 14, 36, 62
2:10-13 53
2:11............................4, 47
2:13............3, 36, 37, 38, 45
2:13-15 ....ix, 1, 35, 36,
       37, 45, 77
2:14..........4, 6, 9, 14, 36, 38,
       39, 40, 45, 52, 53, 54
2:14-15 ....31, 35, 53, 54
2:15........5, 6, 14, 30, 32, 36,
       37, 45, 46, 47, 52, 53, 61
2:16....................................5
2:17....................................5
2:18................................5, 6
2:19....................................6
2:20............................5, 62
2:23....................................5
3:3....................................38
3:4..............................38, 70
3:5-7 3
3:9....................................47
3:11..............................3, 5

4:7......................................3
4:11................................3, 5
4:12....................................2
4:13....................................2

1 Thessalonians
1:10..................................16

1 Timothy
2:5................................ 49

Philemon
23......................................2

Hebrews
11:35..............................16

1 Peter
1:18..................................62
1:19..................................62

1 John
3:5....................................40
5:19..................................60

Revelation
11:15..............................67
12:10..............................67

Author Index

Abbot, T.K., 38, 79
Aland, B., Alan, K., Karavidopoulos, J., Martini, C.M., and Metzger, B.M., 79
Allen, C.J., 2, 83
Aulén, G., 7-8, 9, 10, 15, 79

Bank, R., 31, 81
Beare, F.W. and MacLeod, G. P., 3, 79
Boyd, G., xiii, xiv, 15, 17, 31, 32, 60, 61-62, 72-73, 79
Bratcher, R.G. and Nida, E.A., 40-41-42, 45, 47, 49, 50, 79
Bruce, F.F., xiv, 2, 3, 4, 7, 11, 12-14, 15, 17, 21, 24-25, 26, 27, 28-29, 30-31-32-33, 35, 37, 44-45, 49, 51, 55, 62-63, 69, 70, 71-72, 79, 83, 84
Burkholder, L., 59, 69, 73, 83
Buttrick, G.A., 3, 79

Danker, F.W., 14, 25, 79
Debelius, 53

Elwell, W.A., 16, 79
Erdman, C.R., 23, 51-52, 80

Fahlbusch, E. and Bromiley, G.W., 16, 80
Farmer, W.R., Moule, C.F.D., and Niebuhr, R.R., 44, 84

Gaebelein, F.E., 22, 25, 36, 82
Garland, D. E., 61, 80
Goodspeed, E., 3
Gunton, Colin, 9, 10

Harrington, W. and Senior, D., 2-3, 82
Hooker, M.D., 4

Jeremias, J., 43, 80

Keener, D., 73, 83
Kiley, M., 70, 80, 81

Ladd, G.E., 61, 66, 80
Leivestad, R. 35-36, 42-43, 46-47, 52-54, 80, 81
Lightfoot, J.B., 5, 24, 39, 45, 47, 48, 80
Lincoln, A.T. and Wedderburn, A.J.M., 70-71, 80

MacGregor, G.H.C., 67, 83
Maclaren, A., 49, 80
McIntyre, J., 9
Mansfield, M.R., 28, 37-38, 84
Martin, R.P., 12, 31, 36-37, 61, 80, 81
Metzger, B.M., 27, 37, 81
Mitton, C.L., 70, 81
Moule, C.F.D., 24, 41, 43-44, 45, 81, 84
Moule, H.C.G., 5, 6, 38, 39, 47-48, 49, 52, 81

Nash, J.M., xiii, 84

O'Brien, P.T., 30, 81

Percy, E., 53, 81
Pickell, C.N., 3, 43, 50, 81

Richardson, A, 16, 17, 81
Richardson, A. and Bowen, J., 82
Rienecker, F., 39, 82
Robertson, A.T., 38, 41, 42, 45, 50, 82
Robinson, J.A.T., 47
Rogers, Jr., C.L., 39, 82
Rogers, Jr., C.L. and Rogers, III, C.L., 24, 82
Rogers, P.V., 2, 22, 82

Schweitzer, E., 22-23, 84
Stagg, F., xiii, 11-12, 32, 82
Stevens, B.A., 69, 84
Stott, J.R, 10, 11, 33, 35, 37, 43, 46, 49, 51, 54-55, 63-65, 66, 67, 74, 80, 82

Taylor, V., 31, 82
Tidball, D., 2, 8, 9-10-11, 12, 15, 28, 29-30, 65, 74-75, 82
Twerski, A.J., xiii, 82

Vaughn, C., 2-3, 4-5, 6, 22, 24, 25-26-27, 36, 81, 82
Voorwinde, S., 66, 67, 70, 74, 80, 84

Weaver, J.A., 22, 23, 84
Webber, R.E., 83
White, R.E.O., 2, 3, 5, 6, 83
Wilson, G.B., 4, 7, 39, 40, 41, 42, 43, 49-50, 83

Yates, R., 5-6, 83
Yeager, R.O., 40, 83

Subject Index

Addiction or bondage, xiv, 1, 7, 16, 17
  every other form of, 62
  evil, spiritual world, 61
  law, sin, and death, 61
  of the enemy, 60
  principalities, 5, 32, 37, 46, 50, 51, 52, 53, 55, 61, 64, 71
  principles, 61, 62
  redeeming persons out of this, 62
  spiritual beings or forces, xiii, 1, 7, 14, 17, 26, 47
    as intermediaries, 26
    evil, ix, xiv, 17, 26, 77
    forbidden to worship, 21
    good, xiv
    oppress, xiii
    possess, xiii
  spiritual powers, 5, 51
  unseen powers, 75
Addictions, xiii, 1
  impersonal forces, 1, 17, 61, 63
  defeated forces, 49, 63
  impersonal powers, 61
  inimical forces, 63
  invisible forces, 75
  oppressing forces, 64
  personal or spiritual beings, xiii, 1, 17
    prince of the power of the air, 63
Ambrose, 48
Angelic agencies, 52
Angelic beings, 51
Angels, 5, 29, 49, 50, 52
  bad, 49
  good, 49, 52
  twelve legions of, 51
Atonement, 7, 8, 9, 10, 16, 59
  as cosmic drama, 9
  classic idea, 7, 8, 10
  dramatic idea, 7, 9
  of Jesus, 9
  of reconciliation between God and the world, 8, 9
Atonement theories, 59
  Christus Victor, 7, 59
  Legal Satisfaction, 59
  Moral Influence, 59
Augustine, 48
Baptism (buried with Christ), 61
  set free from personal or impersonal powers, 61
Believers, 7, 13, 14, 29, 39, 60, 62, 63, 64, 65, 70, 74, 75
  are now in stage five, 65
  are only complete in Christ's fullness, 7
  lives are hidden with Christ in God, 70
  on the Lord's side in the conflict of the ages, 70
  reconciled to God through him, 12, 13, 14, 32, 70, 71
  victory is seen in the lives of, 70
Bond, 40, 41, 42,
Calvary, 16
Canceling, 55, 41, 46
  a bond, 41,
  and removing it, 46
Cancelled, 39, 40, 41, 42, 45, 51
  a debt, 51
  having, 39, 45
Captives, 48
Cast aside forever, 47
Christ, 1, 49, 50, 51, 52
  ambassadors for, 69
  and His sufficiency, 36
  as agent in reconciliation, 10, 13, 21
  as Conqueror, xiv, 7-10, 15, 35, 37, 39, 46
  as Conqueror: Colossians 2:13-15, 37-54
  as Conqueror: Colossians 2:14, 39-45

Christ as Conqueror and Reconciler

as Conqueror: Colossians 2:15, 46-54
as Creator, 22, 23, 27, 32, 50
as crucified, 26, 52, 59, 65, 67, 69, 79
as Crucified One, 43, 59
as forgiver: Colossians 2:13, 11, 37-39
as fullness of deity dwelling in, 6, 24, 25
as head over all rule and authority, 36, 62
as headship over all things in status, 6
as His body, 47, 48, 70
as life, 7, 52, 63
as Lord, 49, 63, 64, 67
as mediator between God and the world, 26
as preeminent in all things, 22
as Reconciler, xiv, 10-14, 15, 21, 27, 35, 77
as Reconciler: Colossians 1:19-20, 21-33
as risen, 39, 49
as Savior, 51, 60
as Supremacy in creation over all things, 6
   including authorities, 6, 30, 46, 47, 50, 52, 61, 71
   including powers, 6, 30, 36, 43, 47, 49, 50, 51, 53, 54, 61, 66, 67, 74
   including rulers, 6, 29, 31, 46, 47, 50, 61, 71
   including thrones, 6, 31
as the Son and Image of God, 21
as triumph, 7, 8, 10, 14, 36, 48, 49, 51, 52, 53, 66, 67, 75
as true head and fount of life and knowledge, 7
atoning work of,
   cosmic perspective, 53
caused himself to no longer be under the power of, 47
hands over the kingdom to God the Father, 67
has abolished all rule and authority and power, 61
in Christ, 13
in principle bought persons out of every other form of bondage, 60-62
purpose of his mission -- destroy every rule and every authority and power 61
their life is manifested, 70
to reconcile all things to himself through Christ, 26, 27, 28, 33
victor, 7, 49, 51, 59
   defeated Satan and his hosts, 51
   dragging foes at the wheels of his triumphal car, 49
   parading foes as his captives, 49
   stripping his foes of arms, 49
   stripping his foes of dress, 49
   stripping his foes of ornaments, 49
victories
   over enemy, 59
victorious, 8, 36, 43, 49, 61, 63, 73, 77
victory, 7, 10, 35, 37, 49, 50, 51, 52, 53, 54, 59, 60, 63, 64, 65, 66, 67, 70
   begun during his public ministry, 51
   final ... is yet to be gained, 66
   is humankind's, 43, 50
   over all things through the cross, 6
   over cosmic powers, 54, 61
   over evil, 7
   over evil powers, 69
   over the demonic, 10
   predicted after the Fall, 51
victory procession, 49

Subject Index

as though marching in
triumph, 49
put Satan and his hosts to
open shame, 51
showing that he has
conquered powers or
spirits, 49
work of, 16
Christ's death, ix, 11, 30, 49, 59,
67, 77
resulted in new relationship
between God and
humankind, 11
Christ's death and resurrection, 59,
60
cleansing and restoring work—a
result, 59
final transfer of sovereign, 59
the previous ruler of this world
has been driven out, 60
Christians, 60, 61, 62, 63, 64, 66,
72, 73
are liberated because the whole
universe has in principle been
liberated from the evil one,
60
are made alive together with
Christ, 64
are made complete in Christ, 7,
62
are reconciled to God because
the whole universe has in
principle been reconciled to
him, 60
as all things are under Christ's
feet, 32, 64
they are under Christian's
as well, 64
can now resist their enemies and
walk in freedom, 65
for Christians as for Christ, 63
life means also victory, 63
life means conflict, 63
right to share his throne as
Christ shared his father's
throne, 63

have a victory to celebrate and
proclaim with assurance, 65
have the same power over them
that Christ himself has, 62
overcome the evil one, 63, 64
raised us up with him (Christ),
64
seated us with him (Christ) in
heavenly places, 64
victory of, 64
Christological hymn, 14, 21
Christ as agent of God in
creation of the universe, 21,
23
is good, 22
not dualistic, 22
first-born of all creation, 22,
23, 27
fear not nor worship, 22
goal of the whole creation is
in Christ, 23
made of matter and spirit, 22
over it in rank and dignity,
22
priority in time, 22
world is where humanity
finds authentic existence,
22
Christ as agent of God in
reconciliation, 21, 27
Christ as conqueror, 14
Christ as his redeeming work,
23
Christ as reconciler, 14
Christ having made peace
through the blood of the
cross, 28
Christ holds all things together,
22, 23
Christ is pre-eminent in all
things, 22, 23
Christ is the firstborn from the
dead, 22
Christ is the head of the Church,
22, 23
Christology, 6, 69

of cosmic magnitude, 6
Chrysostom, 48
Church, ix, xiv, 2, 3, 4, 12, 17, 22, 23, 48, 52, 65, 67, 69, 70, 71, 72, 73, 77
  assigned an important role at the heart of the revelation of the mystery of God's intention for the universe, 70
  does this through the Spirit, 73
  early church, 69
    Christology of, 69
  enters the battle with assurance, 70
  equipped with his armor, 70
  is God's masterpiece of reconciliation, 71
    the rulers and the authorities in the heavenly places are to learn the manifoldwisdom of God, 71
  is the means by which work is still to be done, 72
  it is comprised of those individually reconciled to God 71
  it misses the cosmic dimension of the church's calling to revolt against all forms of evil, 72
  misses the cosmic aspect of evil, 72
  spiritual warfare of the, 70
  take on and overthrow evil powers just as Jesus himself did, 73
Churches, xiv, 1, 2, 4, 63
  in the Lycus Valley, 2, 3, 4
  mainline Protestant, xiv, 1
Code, 43, 55
  nailing it (code) to the cross, 55
  written, with its regulations, 43
Colossae, 2, 4, 49
Colossian Church and heresy, 2-7, 17
  Colossian errorists, 26

Colossians heresy, 2-7, 17, 36, 52
  composition of heresy, 5
  dangerous heresy, 3, 4
  different views concern heresy, 3-5
  founding date, 2
  heresy, 3, 5
  mainly, Gentile 3
  work of Epaphras, 2
Colossian error, 4, 6, 26
  combined Jewish practice with pagan speculation, 4
  form of syncretism, 4
  modification of Jewish Essenes, 5
  to distort and deny the uniqueness of the exalted Lord, 6
  to loosen a person's hold on Christ, 6
  to undermine the gospel, 4
Colossians, 2, 4, 28, 29
  Pauline authorship, 2
  when written, 2
Colossians 2:8-15, 14
  admonitory, 36
  affirmative, 36
  completeness of the believers, 7
  baptism, 37
  circumcision, 37
  new life in the resurrection, 37
Colossians 2:13-15, ix, 35-55
Colossians 2:14-15, 31, 35, 39-55
Colossians and Ephesians, 2-3, 72
  companion epistles, 2-3
  difference between the two, 3
  Pauline authorship of both, 3
  prison epistles, 3
  similarity of both, 3
Conquers hosts of evil, 50
Consummation of the ages, 65, 67, 77
  oppressing forces totally destroyed, 65
Cosmic murder, 59
Cosmic overthrow of the principalities, 37

Subject Index

Cross, xiv
  as a divine and human drama, 10
  as a triumph, 10
  as a work of reconciliation, 11
  as reconciliation itself, 11
  as reconciling all things, 29, 55
  blood of the, 16, 55
  could have come down from for believers, 51
  anthropocentric and cosmic dimensions, 62
  guarantees their (oppressing forces) defeat, 65
  obedient to death on the, 50
  of Christ,
    as reconciliation, 11
  procession of captives, 49
  triumphed over God's enemies, 62
  triumphing over the powerless powers by the, 49
  victory is gained on the, 10, 53
  victory over their enemies through the, 65
Cross and resurrection, xiv, 67
Crucified, 10
  dramatic triumph, 36, 43, 49, 53, 63
  was a conqueror, 10
Crucified in weakness, 51
Crucifixion of Jesus,
  death by, 17
Death of Christ,
  a glorious triumph, 51
  cancelled a debt, 51
  defeat of these powers, 61
  manifested might, 51
  not only a pardon, 51
  on the cross, 42
    reconcile all things to himself, 26, 27, 28, 33
    victorious over all his enemies, 61, 70
  triumph over cosmic powers, 8, 49, 52, 53, 54, 61
Debt of humankind, 40, 41, 42, 43, 51, 53

Decrees stood against us, 39, 41
Defeatists see only the fearsome malice of the devil, 66
Definition of terms, 15-17, 18
  Deliverance, 15-16
  Καταλλαγή, 16
  Salvation, 17
  Salvation as deliverance, 17
  Spiritual forces, 17
Degraded them, 66
Deliverance, xiv, 1
  already been secured, 63, 69
  authority to set people free, 60
  Church's role in, xiv, 1, 7, 69-75
  cosmically, ix, 1, 15, 77
  individually, ix, 1, 15, 77
  coherent with the essence of God's, 59
  diversity in how deliverance is carried out, 73
  saving and cleansing work in creation, 59
  form of ministry, xiv, 59
  form of treatment, 1
  freedom and creativity in the act of 73
  from bondage, xiv
  from forces he (Christ) has overcome, ix, 17, 63
  from sin, 16
  from the works of the devil, 16
  ministry mandated to continue today, 69, 77
  relationship with God rather than technique, 73
  through the power and guidance of the Holy Spirit, 73
  united to Christ, 50
    by faith, 17
    to share his victory here and now, 63
    through baptism, 61
Deliverance healing, 59
Despoil, 50
Despoiled, 58

the principalities and the powers, 51
Despoiled foes, 48
  of their armor, 51
Devil, 16, 50, 51, 62, 63, 64, 66
  believers are set free from, 61
  Christ has already conquered the, 49
  conceded not defeat, 64
  demons of possession, 52
  fight and conquer the, 63
  has been defeated, 50, 64
  has been toppled, 64
  has not yet been destroyed, 64
  with hostile intent, 51
Dibelius, 53
Did away with it, 42
Disarmed,
  as captives, 48, 49
  as strong man, 64
  foes, 48
  principalities, 46
  "shown" in triumph, 48
  the authorities, 46
    spiritual, supernatural, powers, 50
    triumphing over them, 61
  the powers, 43
  the rulers, 46
    spiritual, supernatural, powers, 50
    triumphing over them, 46
Disobedience of one man, 50
  Many were sinners, 50
Diverse elements, 5
  Jewish teaching, 5
  pagan speculative elements, 5
Dualistic nature of *Christus Victor*, 8
  as Atonement, 7, 8
  as relationship of reconciliation, 8
Enemies, 52, 61, 77
  authority of the darkness, 52
  exhibit, 48
  exhibiting, 49
    as the powerless powers, 49
    made a public spectacle, 49

of redemption and the redeemer, 52
  to cast off, 48
  under his feet, 61, 64
  victory over his, 70
  will become his footstool, 67
"Enlightened" worldview, xiii
Enlightenment, xiv
Epaphras
  convert of Paul, 2
  fellow bond-servant of Paul, 2
  fellow prisoner of Paul, 2
Erase, 40
Evil can be defeated in one's life, 60
  because the evil one in principle has been conquered, 60
Exceptional piety, 6
Exegetical and theological perspectives, xiv, 1, 15, 21
Forgiveness of sins, 37, 40, 46, 60, 72
Freedom of believers
  died with Christ to elemental principles
    of the world, 62
  full and unrestricted, 62
Fullness, 23, 24, 25, 33
  all the fullness to dwell in him (Christ), 24, 25, 26, 33, 55
  God himself in all his ... was pleased to dwell, 25, 28
  of Christ, 24, 55, 77
  of Deity, 6, 14, 24, 25
    could bring about reconciliation, 27
    dwells in bodily form, 25
    full measure of, 14, 25
    nothing of ... is lacking in Christ, 25
  of God, 21, 24
    was pleased to dwell, 25
    of him who fills all in all, 24
    was well pleased to take up residence in him, 25
The fullness of God in Christ the forgiver and Conqueror, 35-55

Subject Index

the Reconciler, 21-33
Gnosticism, 5, 6-7
  ascetic withdrawal, 22
  asceticism, 5
  incipient form of, 5
Gnostics, 50
God
  be reconciled to, 12
  dwelling in him (the fullness of), 55
  reconciles the world to himself, 7, 8, 9
  reconciling himself to humankind, 11
  showed his power openly, 52
  weakness of ... stronger than any other force(s), 51
  who reconciled us to himself through Christ, 12, 14, 27
  willed in Christ all fullness should dwell, 24
  working through him (the fullness of), 55
God in Christ, 13, 26, 36
  discarded them, 46
  is in the process of reconciling the world to himself, 14
  of their dignity and might, 46
  reconciling the world to himself, 7, 8, 9, 13, 27, 69
  "stripped" them from self, 46
  stripping them of the badge of their rank, 47
  stripping them of their arms, 47
  unclothed the powers, 47
  was reconciling, 13
God's forgiveness, 17
Goodspeed, 3
Gospel ministry, xiv, 15
Gunton, 9, 10
Handwriting in decrees, 41
Having blotted out, 40
Having forgiven, 38, 40
Hilary, 48
Hooker, 4
Hort, 5
Hymn, 14, 21, 22, 23, 28, 29, 36, 45
Illustration
  battlefield, 53
  battle-scene (no), 53
  beaten enemy of his arms, 53
  public humiliation of high officials, 53
  royal court, 53
Introduction, 1-18
I owe you, 40
Jesus
  and his early disciples, xiv
  became obedient to death, 50
  death of
    caused by the law, 54
    drove out the cosmic murderer, 59
    mystical conflict and victory clearly seen, 52
  drives out evil spirit, 66
  execution of
    as a lawful act (no), 50
    giving of himself in love for others, 50
  grappled with them (evil powers), 51
  healing and deliverance ministry of, 59
    initial victories over the enemy, 59
  kingdom victory, 67
  mastered them (evil powers), 51
  messianic self-understanding of, 69
  over-came evil with good, 50
  overcame the devil, 50
  raised from the dead, 63, 64
  refused to disobey God, 51
  refused to emulate the world's use of power, 51
  refused to hate his enemies, 51
  resisting the devil's temptations, 50
  seated at the right hand of the father, 64
  tempted to shun the cross, 50

vicarious punishment of, 43
victory over death
  eschatological, 59
  not yet fully known, 60
Jewish Essenes, 5
Jewish-Gentile controversy, 3
Jewish rites and ceremonies, 51
Jews and Gentiles, 13, 29
Kaphar, 16
Kingdom of God
  already, 66
  final outcome and triumph certain, 66
  has not been consummated, 66
Kingdom of his beloved Son, 72
Kingdom of Satan
  deliverance of humans from, 72
  is defeated, 73
  rescuing persons out of this, 62
Law
  abolish, 42
  abolished by Christ, 44
  abrogation of the, 53, 54
  as enemy, 9
  broken, 43
  cannot be accountable for his death (directly), 54
  Christ abolished in His flesh, 44
  Christ, the end of the, 43
  Christ, the fulfillment of, 44
  condemnation of, 44, 54
  curse of the, 9, 48, 54
  God's, 41, 43
  legalistic sense of, 43
  Mosaic, 42, 43, 53, 54
  of commandments, 44
  revelatory sense of, 43, 45
  termination of, 44
  verdict of the, 43
Leader—a legitimate ruler, 60
  former ruler held humanity in misery, sin, and bondage, 60
  new leader offers repentance and forgiveness of sin at no cost, 60
Lohmeyer, 53

Lord
  atoning death of the, 52
  did strip his foes for himself, 48
  divided the spoils, 48
  manifest the loving creator God, 22
  of all, 63
  of creation, 22
  ransom of his church, 52
  glorification as its head, 52
  takes from them the armour (sic), 48
  triumph over them (evil powers), 52
  in his resurrection, 52
Lord Jesus Christ
  victory through, 64
McIntyre, 9
Messiah is armed with
  gospel of peace, 74
  righteousness, 74
  truth, 74
Nailed it to the cross, 39, 41
Nailing Christ to the cross, 43
Nailing it to the cross, 41, 42, 55
Naturalistic perspective, xiii
Naturalistic therapy, xiii
Obedience of one man, 50
  many will be made righteous, 50
Origen, 9
Out of the midst, 41
Pacification, 32
Paul , 2, 3, 4, 6, 7, 11, 12, 13, 14, 16, 21, 23, 25, 26, 27, 28, 29, 30, 31, 32, 33, 35, 36, 37, 38, 39, 40, 41, 43, 44, 46, 49, 50, 53, 61, 62, 70, 71, 72, 74, 75
Pauline, 16, 54, 70
Peace, 12, 13, 16, 28, 30, 32, 41, 55, 74
  relationship between believing Jews and Gentiles, 13
  with God through our Lord Jesus Christ, 12-13
Peake, 5

Subject Index

Peleta, 15
Peshito Syriac version, 48
Philosophy, 5
Pilate, 51
Postmodernity, xiv
Problem, xiii, xiv, 1, 17, 18, 31
Purposes of the study, xiv, 1, 15, 17
  primary, 1
  secondary, 1
Rationale for the research, 14-15, 18
  full measure of deity in 2:9 and 1:19, 14, 25
  position taken for this study, 15
  possibly similar forces in 1:16 and 2:15, 14, 35
  the cross as the event for reconciliation and triumph in 1:20 and 2:15, 14
  the unchanged verb "to reconcile" in 1:20 made clearer in 2:10, 14, 15, 14
  various positions on interpretation of selected passages, 15
Reconcile (to), ix, 16, 26, 27, 28, 33, 77
  God through death of his Son, 12
  is parallel to Greek word for dwell, 26
Reconciliation, 8, 10, 11, 12, 13, 14, 16, 21, 23, 24, 26, 27, 28, 29, 30, 31, 32, 35, 37, 71, 77
  as the 'chief theme' or 'centre' of Paul's missionary and pastoral thought and practice, 12
  as interpretative key to Paul's theology, 12
  as progression in Paul's development of the theme, 12
  extends outwardly to the circumference of the gospel, 12
  goes to the heart of New Testament doctrine of salvation, 12
  has committed to us the word of, 69
  have now received the, 12
  leads into the heart of the gospel, 11
  ministry of, 12
  of believers, 13, 14, 29
  is a completed work, 14
  of evil forces, 69
  of evil powers, 31, 46, 69, 73
  of hostile powers, 8, 14, 32, 35, 43, 75
  of humanity to God, 27, 28, 29, 30
  of the universe, 27, 32
  of the world, 7, 8, 9, 13, 29, 69
  is a continuous process, 13-14
  relates to a range of experiences and duties in the Christian life, 12
  word of, 12, 69
Reconciling all things to himself, 55
  reconciling of God to himself, 8
  reconciling repentant and believing sinners, 29
  reconciling the world to himself, 13, 14, 29, 69
Record of debt, 39, 40
Redemption, 6, 16, 32, 45, 52, 62, 67, 72
  accomplished by Christ on the cross, 45
  cosmic redemption will be complete, 67
  price of, 62
  with precious blood ... of Christ, 62
  the nature of this redeeming work ... Christ, 23
  to all creation, 16, 27
Resurrecting us with Christ, 55
  share also his throne, 63, 64
Salvation, 6, 8, 9, 12, 17, 71, 72, 74
  a cosmic event, 17
  as deliverance, 17

liberation of the whole world, 17
through the cross and passion, 17
Satan, 51, 59, 60, 62, 63, 66, 67, 72, 73
  Authority, 52, 67
  demons under the power, 63
  has been bound, but not demolished, 66
  his evil dominion, 67
  power of, 63
    has been weakened, 66
  slaves to, 62
Satan and his minions, 62, 67
  destroyed in the same act that destroyed them, 62
  finally destroyed, 67
Satan's stronghold, 60
  in principle has been tottered, 60
  mortally wound and bound, 60
  strong man has been tied up, 60
Secular realm, xiv, 1
Set aside (He), 45
Six stages of God's program, 65
  stage one is the conquest predicted, 65
  stage two is the conquest begun, 65
  stage three is the conquest achieved, 65
  stage four is the conquest confirmed, 65
  stage five is the conquest extended, 65
  stage six is the conquest consummated, 65
Sovereignty, 7, 59
  is universal, 7
Spiritual warfare, 70, 74
  Church is involved in, 70
  of the messianic community, 74
  put on the full armor of God, 74
  spiritual conflict is portrayed, 73
Strange powers, 6

Angels, 5
be placated and worshiped, 6
conquering, 46
degradation of the powers, 53
demonic powers, 62
divine triumph, 53
  over cosmic powers, 53
elemental spirits of the universe, 36, 54
elements of the world, 5
evil powers, 7, 8, 9, 31, 46, 69, 73
hostile powers, 8, 9, 14, 32, 35, 43, 48, 51, 75
moral victory over the powers of evil, 51
  by his love, 51
  by his meekness, 51
  by his obedience, 51
opposing powers, 8
powers of darkness, 66
powers of evil, 8, 46, 48, 49, 51
principalities and powers, 5, 32, 37, 46, 50, 51, 52, 53, 55, 64
  as governments and the authorities, 52
  disarming them, 51, 55
  triumphing over them, 49, 51, 55, 61
  triumphing over them, 49
    by it (the cross), 49, 51, 55
    in him (Christ), 55, 61
  spirits, 49, 53, 61
    evil, 61
    good, 61
satanic power, 66
stood between the believer and God, 6
supernatural powers, 25, 26, 50
the "tyrants", 7
thought they were being victorious, 43
Strip off, 46
  having put off from himself his body, 48, 50

Subject Index

having stripped off, 46
Stripped himself, 47
Stripping for himself, 48
Stripping from himself, 48
    Lord's stripping from himself, 48
Suffering, 7
Summary and conclusion of chapter 3, 54-55
Summary and conclusion of chapter 4, 67
Summary and conclusion of the study, 77
Summary of chapter 1, 17-18
Summary of chapter 2, 33
Summary of chapter 5, 74-75
Take off, 46
Taken it out of the way, 41
Textual problems, 27, 37
Theodore of Mopsuestia, 48
Theological implications for deliverance, xiv, 59-67
To bear, 41
To declare that it is no longer valid, 40
To lift up, 41
To take away, 41
To tear up, 40
To throw away, 40
Torn off, 47
Triumph (in His), 48
    Stripped or cast them off, 48
Triumphalism, 65
Triumphalists, 66
    see only the decisive victory of Jesus Christ, 66

Universal, 26, 27, 30, 31, 52, 59, 70
    ascribing ... supremacy to Christ in his work of reconciliation, 26
Universalism, 32
Versions of the Bible
    ASV, 26
    BrCL, 45
    NEB, 46
    NIV, 46
    RSV, 25, 45
    SpCL, 45
    TEV, 45, 50
    UNASB, 1
Western culture, xiii
Wey, 45
Wipe out, 40
Wisdom, 5, 71, 72
    cosmic before it was anthropological, 72
    God's manifold, 72
    the very wisdom Christians are to proclaim, 72
    the wisdom of Christ, 72
    the wisdom of God in a mystery, 71
    to the principalities and authorities, 71
World, 5, 6, 7, 8, 9, 11, 13, 29, 30, 51, 60, 69
    of creation, 6, 13
    of humanity, 13
    whole human race, 13
Yahweh as a Divine Warrior, 69
Yesu'a, tesu'a, 15

About the Author

DR. JAMES E. NORWOOD, SR., is a Charismatic Baptist minister, teacher, and counselor, with a very diverse educational background and multiple career paths. He graduated from Alcorn State University, Lorman, Mississippi, with a Bachelor of Science degree in biology. He received his Master of Divinity degree in theology from the Southern Baptist Theological Seminary, Louisville, Kentucky. He holds two other master's degrees—a Master of Arts in clinical psychology from Fisk University/Meharry Medical College, Nashville, Tennessee; and a Master of Arts in biblical literature from Oral Roberts University, Tulsa, Oklahoma. He earned the Doctor of Education degree in human development counseling from Peabody College of Vanderbilt University, Nashville, Tennessee. The author sees *life* as the common thread holding all of these areas of study together.

Prior to coming to Oral Roberts University, Dr. Norwood taught band music, mathematics, science, and biology in public schools in Liberty, Mississippi; South Bend, Indiana; and Louisville, Kentucky, respectively. He has also taught Bible, Greek, and theology at American Baptist College and Simmons College of Kentucky for a total of twelve years. He has served as pastor of three churches in Michigan, Kentucky, and Tennessee; as chaplain in two different correctional facilities; and as a professional counselor for a number of years.

Christ as Conqueror and Reconciler

Dr. Norwood remains very active in his local church, serving as the founder, educator, and one of the prayer sharers of the church's prayer ministry. He also teaches a Sunday school class, speaks, and counsels.

Although he has accomplished much academically and professionally, Dr. Norwood is especially respected and admired at ORU for his gentle spirit, wisdom, and the time that he gives generously as Director of Student Development. In that role, he tries to see the "person" in each student.

In his leisure time, Dr. Norwood enjoys reading and playing the piano and organ. For outside activities, he likes to swim, walk in wooded areas, observe the beauty of nature, and listen to its sounds.

www.ingramcontent.com/pod-product-compliance
Ingram Content Group UK Ltd.
Pitfield, Milton Keynes, MK11 3LW, UK
UKHW041448180426
11946UKWH00001B/4